Liberating Voices/Liberating Minds

is a book series of youth writings and curriculum developed, published, and distributed by **The Brotherhood/Sister Sol**. Liberating Voices/Liberating Minds also includes professional development trainings for community and school-based educators.

• • • • •

Off the Subject: The Words of Lyrical Circle of The Brotherhood/Sister Sol
A collection of poetry and spoken word pieces from the award-winning youth collective, Lyrical Circle. Foreword by SEKOU SUNDIATA. Afterword by NIKKI GIOVANNI. Edited by Khary Lazarre-White.

Brother, Sister, Leader: The Official Curriculum of The Brotherhood/Sister Sol
Educational strategies, Rites of Passage Program activities, plus 50 workshops for helping middle and high school students explore critical social issues and develop leadership skills. Compiled, edited and designed by Susan Wilcox.

Voices of The Brotherhood/Sister Sol
An anthology of youth essays, poetry, reflections, and commitments developed over six years of conducting the Rites of Passage Program. Foreword by SEKOU SUNDIATA. Edited by Khary Lazarre-White.

• • • • •

The Brotherhood/Sister Sol (BHSS), co-founded by Khary Lazarre-White and Jason Warwin, is a nonprofit community organization based in Harlem offering comprehensive educational and leadership programs that help Black and Latino/a youth develop their individual and collective potential. Its innovative, holistic curriculum has received national recognition for engaging youth who are achieving significant academic, social, and leadership outcomes.

www.brotherhood-sistersol.org

All net proceeds from the sales of *Why Did This Happen? Content, Perspective, Dialogue: A Workshop Model for Developing Young People's Reflective Writing* support the work of The Brotherhood/Sister Sol (BHSS), a nonprofit community organization based in Harlem and committed to helping Black and Latino/a youth develop into empowered critical thinkers and community leaders. This book was written and designed by Susan Wilcox, and is the intellectual concept of Susan Wilcox, Khary Lazarre-White, and Jason Warwin.

© 2008 by The Brotherhood/Sister Sol

ISBN: 0-9779082-2-4

Book design/layout: Susan Wilcox
Photographs: Brotherhood/Sister Sol staff and members, Ray Llano

The Brotherhood/Sister Sol
512 West 143 Street
New York, NY 10031
212.283.7044
212.283.3700 fax
info@Brotherhood-SisterSol.org
www.Brotherhood-SisterSol.org

A Liberating Voices/Liberating Minds Publication

Why Did This Happen?

Content, Perspective, Dialogue:

A Workshop Model for

Developing Young People's Reflective Writing

Susan Wilcox

For my parents and first liberation teachers
Dr. Katherine Knight Wilcox & Preston Wilcox
• • • • •

CONTENTS

Introduction

In the middle of Harlem in the days following the attack on the World Trade Center on September 11, 2001, different youth members of The Brotherhood/Sister Sol (BHSS) approached our staff wanting to know, "Why did this happen?" Our young people's response to the event was unlike those of some adults they overheard on the street whose immediate thought was that the U.S. should "nuke em." Instead, they were asking their BHSS Chapter Leaders, facilitators of our single-sex **Rites of Passage Program**, for a session that would help them understand the underlying reasons for the attack. Here were young people seeking something educational and referencing the core approach of BHSS that they had come to know and appreciate. This book shares with you our transformative writing and critical thinking approach, the **Content, Perspective, Dialogue (CPD) Workshop Model.**©

Teachers and youth workers, too, are asking for help, wanting to learn strategies for getting their students to write in the ways that they are seeing with BHSS members. During **Liberating Voices/Liberating Minds Institute**, the professional development trainings we conduct around the country, we hear a constant refrain from educators who have been reading through two analogies of our members' writings: *Voices of The Brotherhood/Sister Sol* and *Off the Subject: The Words of Lyrical Circle of The Brotherhood/Sister Sol*. So many talk about working with students who struggle to read, no less write, and we hear in their descriptions qualities of our own members: young people who rarely read, who do not write to reflect, and who do not especially want more "educational" activities after their school day has ended. The implication is that their students are unlike our members, whom they assume are all academically strong. But where many of the educators we meet are struggling with learner apathy, BHSS staff are inspiring middle and high school students to seek content and opportunities to explore and test their ideas. Our staff starts by facilitating workshops on issues they think will interest young people and are important for them to examine (using our *10 Curriculum Focus Issues* as a guide). Our members then begin to see opportunities for learning all around them and ask for workshops on the issues that most matter to them.

How is it that young people's innate desire to learn, so fresh when they enter kindergarten, so often wears away by middle and high school? How is it that youth, who typically have an inherent sense of justice, become apathetic teenagers? **CPD** fills the gulf that lies between the traditionally structured teacher-learner dynamic and young people's knowledge and natural curiosity.

> **ILLUSTRATION**: *BHSS partners with public secondary schools where we establish our Rites of Passage Program and create single-sex chapters. Chapter members participate in a four-to-six-year process of self and community development. One of our members was evaluated academically alongside other students in his school. Tracking his achievement through high school, it was assessed that the elemental difference between this young man's success and his peers was his participation in The Brotherhood. In the same chapter, another young brother was consistently doing poorly in school. Comments on his report card describe a continually restless and disruptive student. But in Brotherhood sessions his thinking flourishes. He peppers chapter discussions with references to news reports and educational television content, and juggles reading several fiction and non fiction books at one time. He is someone who actually knows the difference between Shiite and Sunni Muslims. Where his Brotherhood Chapter Leaders and peers see a young man thirsty for knowledge and interested in wide-ranging social issues, his teachers see a stereotypical young Black man headed in the wrong direction. How is it that his teacher and principal encounter someone so intellectually different from the young people in his Brotherhood community?*

Through the **CPD** Workshop Model, we work to develop in youth a lifelong love of learning and an ability to utilize their knowledge and skills to transform themselves. **CPD** is a living, dynamic writing approach that ignites youth, even those identified by their teachers or principals as being unteachable. We believe that as educators embrace this model in their own settings, even resistant students will become inspired learners.

CPD Components

Content includes information, facts, and experiential activities. It is the common knowledge and experiences a class or group acquires for engaging in informed critique and dialogue. Facilitators carefully select socially salient, diverse, and challenging material that includes literature, essays, and poetry (such as by James Baldwin, Audre Lorde, or Sekou Sundiata), and mainstream media (e.g., *The New York Times*, music videos). They facilitate outings to museums and movies, ethnographic research and community mappings (e.g., young people research and analyze data about aspects of their own or other communities), and arts projects. Content draws young people in, exposes them to myriad ideas and ways of living, and builds on their knowledge, interests, and skills.

Perspective is the lens through which young people critique content. With the West African proverb, "Only when lions have historians will hunters cease being heroes," in mind, **CPD** helps young people learn how to examine points of view (their own and others) and the influences from which they derive. Developing an immersed, coherent perspective comes from being exposed to and reflecting on rich content. It requires listening closely to viewpoints different from your own and realizing that learning is a process of exchange to which everyone has something to contribute. A *Framework for Analysis* (pages 62-63) can guide educators in developing individual or a series of workshops that bring out the relevancy of the topic to youth and to examine it through the concepts of *knowledge of the world*, *unity*, *leadership*, *power*, and *transformation*.

9

Dialogue brings in young people's voices in formal and informal discussion and through reflective writing. Dialogue connects and illuminates content and perspective. When Spike Lee's movie *Bamboozled* came to New York City several years ago, some of our members asked their Chapter Leaders when they would be going to see it. They knew

> It is the synergy of **Content, Perspective** and **Dialogue** —one or two is not sufficient— that makes the Workshop Model unique, and reflective writing is the core tool used for nurturing young people's exploration and expression. **CPD** leads young people to ask their own questions.

it was the *type* of movie BHSS staff would choose because it was written and directed by a person of color and dealt with issues of race and gender that our young people confront each day and explore as part of our curriculum focus. Our members also knew, as well as valued, that the outing would begin with a workshop and end with a reflective discussion and/or writing assignment. Spoken and written dialogue helps young people deconstruct and analyze content and perspective.

It is the synergy of Content, Perspective and Dialogue–one or two is not sufficient–that makes the Workshop Model unique and effective in expanding young people's natural love of learning and their understanding of themselves and the human condition. It gives voice to and helps young people develop their individual creative and intellectual voices, leading them to answer for themselves, "Why did this happen?" Enveloping the model, and key to it being successfully implemented, is young people and adults working together to create a learning environment that nurtures respect, trust and relationship-building. A caring space draws young people into the learning activities and draws out their opinions, beliefs and stories as a result of their feeling supported and safe. The intended outcome is that they perceive themselves as knowledgeable and capable and become committed to learning and to making constructive decisions affecting their lives and those around them.

10

A teen and facilitator at work.

· · · · ·
CPD Core Assumptions

CPD grew out of Brotherhood/Sister Sol's work with middle and high school students participating in our **Rites of Passage Program**. As BHSS expanded, we utilized the same strategies in other programs we offer teens: the **Liberation Program** (for youth organizing and training), **International Study Program** (for developing cross-cultural awareness and global competency), and **Writers' Collective** (for honing skills in writing, poetry, and spoken word).

BHSS members are not handpicked but are representative of the range of students found in most urban schools. Some earn straight A's, and others struggle to pass their classes. Some live in public housing, and others in homes owned by their parents. They are Black American, Dominican, Puerto Rican, Haitian, Jamaican, Guyanese, Ghanaian, and Honduran: a diversity both intentional and a reality of the communities where they live (Harlem, Washington Heights, the South Bronx, Flatbush, Bedford-Stuyvesant). They are "at risk" of receiving an inferior education, of becoming numb to curriculum that has no resonance to who they are and how they live. Each is curious, about some thing, indeed, many things. The challenge for educators working with youth "like BHSS members" is to engage them such that they proactively seek to learn, understand, and become storytellers and historians.

CPD can be utilized by educators working in after school programs or teaching in school classrooms who want to help young people develop competence in critical thinking and writing. The foundation of the Workshop Model rests on nine core assumptions.

1. Teachers and youth workers serve as facilitators. Facilitators provide information and foster critical inquiry so that young people discover answers and identify questions for themselves. Good facilitation practices democratic authority that depends on building trust and views learning as a reciprocal process. Facilitators are not required to have all the answers, but to present information, concepts, and questions that promote critical exploration. They must also cultivate respect between and among youth and adults so that the learning environment becomes one of shared trust. Good facilitation means that *how* information is presented is as significant as *what* is presented.

2. Affirming young people's skills and knowledge instills confidence and courage. To have their thoughts heard and see their words in print is to recognize that their knowledge and perspectives are meaningful. Facilitators need to encourage all young people to participate, to contribute to discussion, or to read their writing, in order to hone their unique voice, and inform others.

3. Two facilitators enhance educational and enrichment activities and group building. When educators collaborate on developing and facilitating workshops and programs, they increase creativity and diverse perspectives to which young people are exposed, can better manage the multiple needs of their group, and provide each other with mutual support.

4. Young people's experiences and backgrounds are essential assets in the learning process. Youth become engaged learners/teachers when they share their stories and connect personal experiences to larger social issues. With guidance they can learn how to facilitate workshops, and their approach will no doubt reveal activities that are especially appealing to youth.

> *"Knowing/realizing how effective and empowering youth work can be makes me feel like I can go back to my organization with a renewed sense of purpose."*
> Liberating Voices/Liberating Minds Institute participant

5. The learning environment matters. It needs to be welcoming to all youth; inclusive of their interests, values, and needs, and safe for them to express their opinions, beliefs, fears, and aspirations. Young people should see their writing, art, and ideas hung on the walls. The setting should be comfortable, ordered, and designed for their age and interests: a space for which they want to take responsibility.

6. Workshop topics and materials need to resonate with young people. In order to be intellectually and socially well rounded it is necessary for young people to explore a vast variety of issues. They are, however, naturally engaged by reading and learning about the experiences of people like themselves and/or about realities similar to their lives, and this is where facilitators should begin.

7. Young people need positive alternatives. Rather than pointing out negative choices and behaviors, young people develop from having access to positive options. This pushes them to articulate what they stand for rather than against, and places decision making in their hands. The result is the increased likelihood that they will seek positive outcomes and practice leadership.

8. Youth desire what many adults forget is so essential: fun. Learning must engage young people's minds, bodies, and spirits. Facilitators should therefore explore ways for energizing young people by using icebreakers and activities that make them think and move. They need to also be attuned to young people's moods and immediate needs and be flexible about modifying activities if necessary.

9. Youth excel when held to high expectations. Facilitators should choose intellectually demanding content, develop challenging activities, help young people make decisions, and hold them accountable to their self-defined beliefs and commitments. These are strategies that help them take responsibility for shaping their life paths.

• • • • •
The Influence of **CPD** on Brotherhood/Sister Sol Members

Eighty-eight percent of BHSS members have graduated from high school, and the percentage rises to 94% when including those earning a General Equivalency Diploma. Eighty-five percent have been accepted to college, and 95% are attending college and/or working. Our members are mentoring, organizing, and serving in leadership positions on their school campuses. A third of BHSS staff are program alumni. Our members are intentionally delaying parenthood. Only three had a child before graduating from high school, with every father having shared or primary custody. None of our members are incarcerated.

By comparison, New York City has a high school graduation rate of about 50%, though for Black and Latino males it is closer to 35%. Their female counterparts are at least twice as likely to graduate. Nationally the graduation rate for Black and Latino/a students is not much better (60%). There are more Black males in U.S. prisons than in classrooms. One in 15 Black males and one in 26 Latino males are currently serving time. Seventy-five percent of state inmates do not have a high school diploma. In the last 10 years the number of women in prison increased by 64% (34% are Black and 16% are Latina). The U.S. teenage birthrate (42 per 1,000 women under age 20) is one of the highest for industrialized nations. In New York City the rate averages 9.4%. The national unemployment rate is around 5%, but in New York City as many as 50% of Black males are without jobs. Insufficient educational opportunity, lack of job skills, a culture of poverty, a sense of hopelessness: each is part of the cycle of unfulfilled potential experienced by too many young Black and Latino/a people.

Reflective writing is obviously not the sole reason for our members' successful outcomes, but it is a primary tool for helping them confront and counteract their social circumstance. Writing has the power to build self-knowledge and support self-determination. (Perceiving self-awareness as a necessary stepping-stone toward realizing personal and social change, a founding Brotherhood chapter chose the name *Knowledge of Self*.) Through writing, some of our members discover a medium for creative expression they will devote themselves to as poets, spoken word artists, and filmmakers. Most, however, will acquire an ability to analyze complex issues, make positive personal choices, and act in socially conscious ways within their families and communities.

Why Did This Happen? Format

Why Did This Happen? describes how **CPD** is implemented and showcases its impact in samples of our members' writing. The curriculum is organized into five chapters, beginning where all work with young people should: with ideas for creating an environment of trust and respect. In the first chapter, **My Grades Do Not Reflect My Intelligence or Personality: Setting the Tone**, the focus is on creating such a space. The second and primary chapter, **Content, Perspective, Dialogue: A Workshop Model**, describes the model's key components and how to utilize it through identifying focus issues, incorporating the *Framework for Analysis*, choosing challenging content, and developing critical questions. **Let My Soul Spit: Nurturing Reflection** examines reflection as an intentional practice and gives strategies for fostering it in young people. **I Want to Always Learn: Incorporating Drafts and Revision** is a guide for helping youth develop skills for and the habit of editing their work. **I Do Not Have Weak Dreams: Providing a Forum** gives suggestions for how and where youth can present, perform, and publish their writing. Within all the chapters are Illustrations (descriptions of real experiences with our members), an entire or excerpted writing sample from BHSS members, Strategies for implementation, and Resources. The first three chapters additionally offer relevant sample Workshops.

Why Did This Happen? contains easy-to-follow original **Workshops** that include easy-to-find **Resources**. Some also provide ready-to-use **handouts**. The workshops are activities for creating a supportive context and/or offer specific approaches for engaging youth in reflective writing. All have been particularly useful for developing young people's knowledge through promoting critical questioning. **Recommended time frames guide facilitators in adapting the workshops to their specific settings and requirements**. Classroom teachers can modify them to fit within a 45-minute to hour-long period, breaking them up into a two-or-three-day (or longer) series. Workshops can be used in Advisory and as an introduction to or featured lesson in a unit of a Humanities, English, History, or art class.

· · · · ·

To see young people grapple with words on paper that results in an impassioned poem about the objectification of women's bodies, or in a letter to a future son advising him how to avoid the temptations of the street, or in any other way strongly articulating their point of view, is deeply gratifying. These are the voices needing, no demanding, to be heard because—and something I have learned from working with young people—they challenge us to continually ask questions and to search for unique and universal truths. How rewarding it is when a young person comes to us asking to know "Why did that happen?" It is the quintessential *a-ha* moment that validates my colleagues and myself as educators.

16

References: *Advocates for Youth* http://www.advocatesforyouth.org; *City Schools and the American Dream, Reclaiming the Promise of Public Education* by Pedro Noguera; *Congressman Charles B. Rangel* http://www. house.gov/rangel/; *Given Half a Chance: The Schott 50 State Report on Public Education and Black Males* www. blackboysreport.org; *Pew Center on the States' Public Safety Performance Project Report 2008,* The Pew Charitable Trust http://www.pewtrusts.org; *Separate and Unequal, the Public School Education Facing Minority Children* prepared by Julian Johnson); *Women in Prison: A Site for Resistance* http://www.womenandprison.org/index. html; *Writing Next: Effective Strategies to Improve Writing of Adolescents in Middle and High Schools* by Steve Grahman and Dolores Perin (Alliance for Excellent Education, Carnegie Corporation of New York); *The U.S. Department of Justice* http://www.ojp.usdoj.gov/bjs/prisons.html; *Young, Gifted and Black: Promoting High Achievement among African-American Students* edited by Theresa Perry, Claude Steele and Asa Hilliard III.

1

My Grades Do Not Reflect My Intelligence or Personality:
Setting the Tone

The one who tells the stories rules the world.
Hopi proverb

Brotherhood/Sister Sol members are academically, economically, and ethnically diverse. We desire this mix of backgrounds, experiences, and skills because it supports our members' learning and echoes real life. Young people see that each of us has something to offer and receive; each of us has strengths and challenges. As much as we appreciate our members' life experiences, we know their school curriculum gives little attention to the issues that matter to them. The history and culture of people of color, women, lesbians, and gays are underrepresented in school lessons and books. There are conversely infinite messages about youth people of color blazing across news headlines and on TV screens that have immediate, visceral impact signifying such stereotypes as thug, teenage parent, and criminal. In too many ways these young people are learning that outside of their families and communities, their lives and those of their ancestors are unrecognizable and unimportant.

17

In public schools in urban areas around the nation, students of color are failing or dropping out at unacceptably high rates. Lack of access to quality teaching and current textbooks, un- or misdiagnosed learning needs, boredom—these are but some of the reasons young people do not thrive, no less excel in school. Common

> It matters that the adults facilitating workshops for youth have respect for their background, knowledge, and interests.

sense suggests that when youth, even those who struggle to read, write, and add, can connect to what they are learning, they are more interested and likely to stay engaged. It also matters that the adults facilitating workshops have respect for their background, knowledge, and interests and are at every step, affirming that they have much to offer and achieve. BHSS staff help young people deconstruct what they are learning and observing toward defining for themselves what it means to be a man, woman, leader, Black, Latino/a, gay, straight, working-class, or middle class. We strive to make clear that although they are inheriting a system of oppression, they come from a rich cultural background that has contributed to the evolution of societies around the world. It is a complex history and not without its faults, but it did not begin with, nor should it be defined by, slavery and its legacy. Their heritage has helped build this nation and shape the world.

ILLUSTRATION: *Brotherhood attended a performance of John Leguizamo's* Freak *on Broadway—a poignant, hilarious, and brutally honest coming-of-age story about a Latino immigrant family trying to make sense of life in America. The brothers laughed all the way through, even at the sad stories because they got at the heart of Leguizamo's struggle toward manhood, while balancing his family's culture with being a New York City kid. Leguizamo introduced the audience to his angry machismo father,* novella-*watching mother, pesky little brother, and his own ambition to hang out on the corner and get a girl. He not only brought us into his home, but into those of many other Latino families. The resonance with Latino Brotherhood members was obviously deeply meaningful in hearing "their" story through Leguizamo's affectionate telling, and in being proud of his achievement in being able to tell it on Broadway. Through strength of voice, a Latino, working-class brother from a "hood" like where our members live had made it to the Great White Way.*

Many young people attend schools where their ideas and opinions are less important than their ability to recall facts, particularly on standardized tests that have been shown to be culturally biased. Consequently we know that when we begin working with a new group of youth, we expect some will find it difficult to accept that it is their thinking we want to hear, their perspectives and honest opinions. Some may be shy, but some have surely been conditioned not to challenge information, to accept the word of their elders wholesale, or at the very least not to contest it, especially if earning a grade is involved. But what happens when young people realize they are in a setting where their opinions and questions matter? Writing provides a space for offering their opinions and is a way into their seeing that their ideas, beliefs, and values matter.

ILLUSTRATION: *Nicholas was cautious when he came to us. He was suspicious of Bro/Sis and hesitant to open up. When he first joined The Brotherhood, during sessions he would only sit and watch, closed off and waiting to see if the organization was "for real." He maintained a blank face and remaining guarded. New to the chapter, brothers admitted that he was the one that, if they didn't know him, they would never mess with. Slowly he began to become comfortable. Once he saw that we lived brotherhood, meaning that the space was respected and his opinion mattered, he began to lend his voice to the dialogue. As he said, he found The Brotherhood inspirational. Once opened, it was a like a torrent had been released. Nicholas had an opinion on everything, earning the title of philosopher, and when his Check-in turn came around he would smile, his eyes glinting as he smacked his hands together, and say, "I'm ready with my 30 minutes." He began to share his view of the world, his opinions, and his deepest thoughts. Our space became a place where he could vent and share. His teachers, who rarely saw inside Nicholas, would be stunned by his voice so uniquely and powerfully manifested in his words and writing. (See Nicholas's essay on page 20.)*

• • • • •

Implementing the **CPD** Workshop Model begins with **Setting the Tone.** Teachers and youth workers convey from the start that the culture, life experiences, knowledge, and interests of young people are central. They demonstrate that their role in the educational process is as facilitator–someone who coordinates activities, helps to move discussions forward, and incorporates young people's ideas and talents into the learning experience. There are times when facilitators provide information and a framework for understanding, perhaps in the form of a short lecture. Overall, however, the facilitator's role is to co-create with young people a space where together they can develop bonds and learn. **Setting the Tone** is the beginning and a perpetual component of **CPD**. The Strategies and Workshops that follow are the first steps.

> Setting the Tone is a continual process.

HARLEM BORN, HARLEM RAISED
Nicholas Peart, Intrinsic Kings Brotherhood Chapter

I am a young man born and raised in Harlem, New York. Currently, my community is becoming more diverse. Harlem is being flooded by many ethnicities, making the once predominately African-American community one in which African-Americans are becoming the minority.

I am a young African-American male who has been subject to random searches by police officers that I feel are unfair and racially motivated. These are authority figures who are supposed to be present to protect my community. I have wondered why there have been so many officers in Harlem which isn't a borough but a small section within the borough of Manhattan. After much thought, I came to the realization that the heavy amount of officers that I see daily are not here to protect my community, but to protect the rising property value in Harlem from people who look like me—young, Pan-African/Latino people.

Random searches by police are just one of the issues I deal with as a young African-American male which could only be understood by others who have experienced this reality. Growing up, I've had no one in my life to talk to about these types of issues with. I lacked a strong male figure in my life; I was raised by my mother and older sister. Although I appreciate them both, I've always yearned for a positive male figure in my life, someone I could relate to, talk to, and vent to. My mother and sister are strong women who did what they could to raise me to be a man but they could only do so much. Being raised by a woman has affected me positively and negatively. I am calm in demeanor and not as aggressive as many young men in my age group, but many of my questions remained unanswered. I struggled with trying to find my true identity and purpose, until I found The Brotherhood/Sister Sol.

The Brotherhood/Sister Sol is a non profit organization dedicated to helping young people develop critical thinking skills, find direction and purpose in life. I am a proud member of the Intrinsic Kings Chapter of this organization and have been greatly influenced by my Chapter Leaders and the elder members of the organization. As a member of The Brotherhood/Sister Sol, I have learned history which is not a part of the Board of Education's curriculum, such as my true ancestry and how certain institutions in society have been against the development and advancement of Pan-Africans and Latinos in America. As a member of this organization, I experienced college trips, retreats (which focused on developing the mind, body, and spirit), and weekly workshops about issues ranging from growing up as an African-American man to the election process, to health and hygiene. The Brotherhood/Sister-Sol has become the strong influential figure that I've needed all of my life. I now have people to look up to, to admire, and to question about the difficulties of life. This organization provided me with a foundation to build on and has been very inspirational.

The Brotherhood/Sister-Sol has also given me the tools to realize why I continued to have difficulty academically no matter how hard I tried and how badly I wanted to do well. They were there to help me pinpoint and reflect on certain things in my life, so that I could ultimately embrace my past and push for a better future. Throughout my high school career, I was always affected by the lack of stability in my life. I felt at times like my mother was too judgmental instead of helpful. I've always been disappointed that my father decided not to be a part of my life, and the adults in my school constantly put me down. I have also had to deal with the violence in my high school, which at times, made it difficult for me to be passionate about schoolwork. I have felt so much pressure as to whether I should stay in school or quit, and my grades reflect this reality. However, my grades do not reflect my intelligence or my personality. Thanks to The Brotherhood/Sister Sol, I have a newfound respect for myself which allows me to endure and overcome the obstacles I encounter when it comes to school.

The Brotherhood/Sister Sol helped me bridge the gap between my childhood and my manhood. This organization has helped me make sense of what I've gone through in the past and has prepared me for my future. Although I am still trying to be a better man every day, I am no longer lost in someone else's definition of what an African-American man should be. I am not the man certain institutions in my neighborhood have tried to make me out to be. Not only have I been able to define myself, but I have a more positive outlook on life and I am excited to find my place in this world. I have been inspired by the strength, vibrancy, and influence of my history, and I am eager to create a history of my own. I have always dreamt of being part of a college community. I believe that it's the type of atmosphere that will help me further develop myself, my thoughts, and my character. I am also eager to take to college what I have learned from The Brotherhood/Sister Sol by participating in many of the student organizations on campus. I now look forward to my future, and I am excited by its possibilities.

HOW *Setting the Tone* SUPPORTS REFLECTIVE WRITING

Reflective writing is an analytical, active activity emerging from a writer's beliefs, knowledge, and experience. An articulation of ideas and a form of self-expression, writing reveals the social, intellectual, political, and spiritual contexts in which the writer is situated. Using the **CPD** Workshop Model, youth continually move between spoken and written DIALOGUE that brings out CONTENT (information, experiences) and PERSPECTIVE (lens of analysis). Spoken and written words work in tandem to create greater understanding and in-depth critique.

Before any workshop, young people must therefore **feel safe to risk exposing themselves**. Whether commenting on a social issue or telling a personal story, they need assurance that their words (spoken in their lingo) will not be judged or ignored.

Each **Setting the Tone** strategy develops clear expectations for listening, questioning, maintaining confidentiality, and offering sensitive critique. Through DIALOGUE, **Setting the Tone** establishes open communication for building connections and intimacy between youth and facilitators. These relationships embolden young people to engage in writing that is truly reflective and to express themselves in a supportive context of shared intent.

• • • • •

STRATEGIES for
Setting the Tone

1. Establish Rules of Conduct youth and facilitators agree to uphold.

The first time a group comes together it is important to define expectations about how its members will interact with one another. If the group will be meeting over time, identifying shared objectives or values is also important. *Rules of Conduct* are about maintaining respect and order, fostering inclusion, and agreeing on common goals. Effective implementation comes from their steady enforcement by facilitators and young people. Rules are bond: they are not to be written and then forgotten. The list need not be long, but it should be meaningful and practical. See an example of a typical *Rules of Conduct* below.

Rules of Conduct

One mic — A reminder that only one person can speak at a time and that s/he should be listened to

Step up/Step back — A reminder to assertive youth that they need to allow opportunity for more reticent ones to speak up

Attack the idea, not the person — A reminder that discussions and disagreements should focus on the issue and not become personal

No side conversations — A reminder to pay attention and not be disruptive, and that side conversations can make speakers feel ignored and disrespected

What is said in the room, stays in the room — A reminder to maintain confidentiality (especially essential for workshops in which young people and facilitators share personal experiences)

Have fun — A reminder that learning should be an enjoyable experience

The process of developing *Rules of Conduct* is simple, though it may take some time to achieve consensus about the list. (Going forward, consensus building provides ongoing opportunity to intensify respect and trust within the group as young people are pushed to consider different ideas and make compromises.) Teachers and youth workers facilitate the creation of the *Rules of Conduct*, but their opinions are also incorporated, indicating to young people that facilitators are not operating outside of the group, but working alongside youth. The process for developing *Rules of Conduct* is:

A. Briefly describe what a *Rules of Conduct* is and why your group will be creating it. Next, elicit ideas from your group by asking:

> *What are some rules we need for working together?*
> *What are our goals as a group? Why have we come together?*
> *How can we ensure that the experience is positive for everyone?*

To ensure all young people have an opportunity to contribute to the conversation, have them explore these questions in **Pair-ups** (teams of two) which then share their ideas with the entire group.

B. Record all of the responses on large paper (or a blackboard or wipe-off board). You can ask youth to raise their hands to contribute an idea or allow them to just call them out. The method should depend on how quickly you can write and how manageable your group is. It may, for example, be more effective with large groups to have young people raise their hands. Here is where it's useful to have two facilitators as one can write and the other can call on youth. Alternatively, and a regular strategy of BHSS, you can ask for a volunteer to record the responses, a task many will enjoy doing.

C. Once a full list has been generated or your group is not offering any new ideas, the next step is to narrow the list down. If the *Rules of Conduct* is too long it will be hard to remember and put into practice. It can be effective and efficient to ask your group to agree on about five to 10 items. Additionally, ask the young people to identify repeated or similar ideas to further narrow the list and have them reflect on the ease or challenge of achieving specific suggestions. For example, not allowing anyone to use the bathroom during a workshop may be unreasonable, while making a rule that it's okay to nap during a "boring" workshop might be setting the bar too low. Through discussion, young people learn to determine the appropriate level of expectation in assessing whether or not they can feasibly uphold rules.

The depth and length of discussion should depend on your group's focus. If young people are gathered for a one-time workshop, it should be a relatively quick process. You can limit the number of rules to the two or three most important ones for the day. If your group will be meeting together over time and the youth do not know each other, it is essential to spend more time developing the *Rules of Conduct* since they will become part of the group's culture through regular use.

D. After the list has been narrowed down and your group thinks it has addressed the most important issues, the finalized *Rules of Conduct* should be written on a clean sheet of paper so that the young people and facilitators can endorse it with their signatures. This step underscores that their words are "bond" or reliable. The *Rules of Conduct* should then be posted in the space where your group meets, serving as a constant reminder for keeping them accountable to their own words; not to uphold them is to therefore be hypocritical.

FROM *Rules of Conduct* TO *Mission Statement*

Within our **Rites of Passage Program**, chapters write collective *Mission Statements* and *Definitions* for *Sister/Brother, Woman/Man* and *Leader* describing the core ideals all members will strive to live by and which become a chapter's guiding tenets. Chapters revisit and refine their statements each year as they mature. They also create a name that captures the unique interests and values of the chapter. Schools that have participated in *Liberating Voices/Liberating Minds Institute* (our professional development initiative) have adopted the single-sex format of our Rites of Passage Program and/or incorporated *Mission Statements* and *Definitions* into their Advisory. Rather than defining "sister", "brother", "woman", and "man", they define "student", "learner" and/or "leader."

* See **Brother, Sister, Leader: The Official Curriculum of The Brotherhood/Sister Sol** to get ideas for implementing rites of passage activities.

2. Facilitate *Check-in*.

BHSS opens all workshops and program gatherings with *Check-in*. *Check-in* enables youth and adults to reacquaint themselves each time they meet and to unwind. Youth use *Check-in* to vent about a bad experience, share exciting news they cannot contain, or express how they are feeling so they can focus on the workshop to come. *Check-in* is how the group continually exposes feelings, brings out common experiences, develops inside jokes, and builds a culture of trust, respect, and sharing. Whatever is offered is not to be judged or shared outside of the circle. *Check-in* is also when group norms are instilled and behaviors can be modeled. Young people practice listening and speaking skills that are key to creating dialogue. The facilitator's role is to guide them toward honest self-expression, help maintain the *Rules of Conduct*, and manage time. Facilitators also check in because it supports and underscores a culture of reciprocity (e.g., learning is a communal endeavor).

Check-in takes place with the group sitting in a circle so that no one their back to another person. The facilitator asks for a volunteer to begin. After s/he has finished speaking, the young person decides which direction around the circle *Check-in* will continue. Each group member, including the facilitator, then has her or his moment to share.

A typical BHSS *Check-in* with 15 youth and two Chapter Leaders is 20 to 45 minutes long. If time is limited, you can set guidelines for how long each person can speak. Young women may initially be more verbally expressive than young men, and *Check-in* is therefore something they readily embrace. Young women are also frequently given little space to express their ideas in their classrooms or families. For this reason, within Sister Sol there is a rule that whomever is speaking is not to be interrupted.

A 3-MINUTE CIRCLE

If your room is not set up for your group to meet in a circle, challenge your students to quietly and quickly (in about 3 minutes) move the desks or chairs into a circle. Give them a few minutes to develop a plan. Say "go" and time them, letting them know when 3 minutes is up. You might choose to give them more time if they are close to finishing. Have them self-assess their performance. With practice and by reinforcing expectations about how the room should be arranged, the young people will soon, and efficiently, rearrange the room without being asked.

Tenth- to 12th-graders who have become more comfortable with each other and better able to articulate their feelings and thoughts have a longer *Check-in* than 7th- to 9th-graders. You can help younger teens develop emotional and intellectual language through careful prompting. Gently push them to specify what they mean by such vague adjectives as *okay*, *fine*, or *good*. An initial prompt could be: *I'd to know more about how you're feeling or what you're thinking. Do you mind sharing more?* (See other prompts in chart below.) In helping young people to become more expressive, you can give examples before *Check-in* begins, offer prompts during *Check-in*, or close *Check-in* with examples to consider for next time. It can also be useful to provide a list of words describing different emotions (e.g., melancholy, uneasy, elated, quixotic), which will also help build your group's vocabulary. Youth generally like to learn and integrate new words into their conversation (as opposed to having to study them for a vocabulary quiz). You should also always observe and listen carefully to youth, not pushing them when they really don't want to or have anything to share.

If a young person says . . .	You can ask . . .
I'm okay.	*What is something you feel good about these days, and why? What is something that is making you feel bad or sad, and why?* Prompting helps young people more clearly and accurately express and identify the source of their feelings.
I'm doing good in school.	*What do you mean by "good"? Can you give an example of an assignment you felt good about? How would you compare your achievement to last year and with where you hope to be next year?* Prompting helps facilitators assess what a young person accepts as "good" with the objective being to foster high standards.
Life sucks and I wish I didn't have to deal with it.	*What is bad about your life these days? What can you do to make things better?* Prompting helps facilitators uncover whether a young person is dealing with a serious issue or just having a bad moment.

At times what young people share during *Check-in* necessitates a longer discussion and/or follow-up. Here again is an example of the value of having two facilitators. A young person may bring up an issue that needs immediate attention (e.g., he describes a dangerous situation at home). It may be inappropriate for the entire group to address, but requires that one facilitator speak with the young person outside of the room while the other facilitator conducts the workshop. (When this is not possible, it is important to follow up with the young person after the session or class ends.) It could also be that several people in the group bring up the same or similar issues. A few years ago Sister Sol chapter members were having difficulty with a math teacher and were at risk of failing his class. It became important for the entire group to spend time discussing and brainstorming a solution to the problem, and required the Chapter Leaders to modify the workshop. There are also times when the entire workshop has to be scrapped in favor of giving time to explore specific problems of youth. On most days, *Check-in* serves its primary purpose of bringing everyone together in preparation for the workshop, as well as informing facilitators of what young people care and are knowledgeable about. Once it has *Check-in* the workshop can begin.

FACILITATING A GUIDED Check-in

A useful approach when introducing **Check-in** is to ask a focus question such as: *What is something you heard in the news that interested you? What is something you hope to accomplish in the coming weeks? What is an ideal day for you?* Or have them complete each of the following: *I feel . . . I want . . . I need . . .*

Conduct individual **Check-ins** during class changes by standing at the entrance to your room and greeting each student as your class walks in. Pay attention to their moods—who is smiling or dragging themselves in—and ask about how their day is going. Pull a young person aside for a moment if you sense she needs to talk. Your conversation may be brief, but will help settle the young person so she can better focus. You can then follow up when the class ends.

Transitions between activities are important as young people shift from a less formal (**Check-in**) to more formal activity (e.g., workshop), or from a light to serious topic. Giving them a few minutes to expend energy will help them to settle down. Acknowledging transitions instills adaptability and teaches that different activities demand different behavior.

3. Create a welcoming and nurturing learning environment.

From the time our members arrive at our brownstone each day to the time they leave, they are at the center of our work. The BHSS brownstone opens at 10:am when staff begins the day creating and preparing activities, maintaining records, making calls, fundraising, and doing other administrative tasks. But as our members begin arriving just after 3:pm, we turn away from our computers and paperwork to give our attention to them. Here are a few of the ways to create a welcoming and nurturing learning environment:

> *Check-in* is when group norms are instilled and behaviors can be modeled.

A Sense of Order: Entering a clean and organized space signals to young people that they are part of a community of caring and responsibility. Books, games, materials, and personal items all have a place. If feasible, snacks should be prepared and available at the same time each day. Let young people know they can have fun within limits (e.g., no running, play music so as not to disturb others). They should also know that helping to maintain a space from which they benefit is their responsibility. BHSS members help out with cleaning (taking out the garbage, vacuuming, loading the dishwasher). Naturally, they can forget to pick up after themselves (or try to avoid cleaning altogether), and materials do get misplaced and damaged. Maintaining order requires constant vigilance on the part of the facilitators and young people.

Greetings & Good-byes: Our members know that they must greet everyone when entering and say good-bye when leaving. Many years ago we posted this policy, but it has since become the heart of BHSS culture that a sign is no longer necessary. Older members model for and remind younger members to offer greetings, as do staff. Taking time to say hello can seem like an absurdly obvious social interaction, but is not always something young people experience during the day. Their school staff and safety officers are more likely to "greet" them with a command (e.g., "Tuck in your shirt." "You're late."). Ask youth about their day, follow up on a previous conversation, make note of a new hairstyle, or ask the cliché question, "What did you learn in school today?" The point is to get them talking and demonstrate that you are genuinely listening. If you sense a young person has something weighing on him, sit and talk about any number of things until he can open up. Showing young people you are happy to see them and regularly taking time with them for no other reason than to catch up makes them feel valued and realize your caring is constant. Each time they enter the space, they will feel as if they have come "home."

Happy Birthday: Birthdays are big deals at BHSS because they honor the individual and give her a moment to receive some shine. On their day, every youth and staff member gets a cake or some special treat (one of the few times we serve sugary food) with candles to blow out. Whoever is around comes together to sing the traditional and/or Stevie Wonder's version of *Happy Birthday to You*, loudly, often off-key, but with much affection. We know this may be the only celebration a young person has on her birthday. You may not be able to buy a cake and candle for each young person you work with, but you can acknowledge their day by having the group sing *Happy Birthday* to them. You could also recognize everyone who is born in the same month. At the start of the school year or program, mark each person's birthday on a calendar and hang it up.

Creating a Youth-Friendly Space: The environment we create with our members enables them to safely explore and grow. In renovating our brownstone we set aside one room as the *Teen Lounge* because we know adolescents like having a space to call their own. (Our youngest members, age six to 11, have their space too. The walls of our *Mind, Body & Spirit Room* are covered with a mural they designed and painted.) The teens understand that staff can enter the Teen Lounge at any time and that all activities are supervised. Yet because it is comfortable (having a wrap-around banquette cushioned with pillows in African print fabric) and reflects their interests (with posters, job announcements, and college pennants from schools our alumni attend), it feels wholly theirs and like a second home. Choose adornments with a youthful aesthetic (such as graffiti-style signs) and that are amusing (such as funny quotes) or provocative (such as a wipe-off board featuring a quote of the day from the young people). Display content and images representative of the ethnic, gender, sexual orientation, and class diversity of your group and their communities. Hang up your *Rules of Conduct*, or if you choose to create them, the group's *Mission Statement* and *Definitions*. And of course, hang up young people's work and words.

$\bullet\ \bullet\ \bullet\ \bullet\ \bullet$

WORKSHOPS

Overview: In different ways, the following workshops were designed for helping young people and adults with **Setting the Tone** for an environment in which knowledge and respect for the backgrounds, experiences, and ideas of all group members can be respectfully exchanged. The first workshop is an introductory activity, the second focuses on re-establishing group ties, and the last presents historical content that connects to present-day media and young people's personal experiences. The workshops in this chapter are:

- o I Feel
- o An Experience I Had That Changed Me
- o Proverbs, Folktales & Fables:
  Oral Tradition From the Root to Today

Brainstorming at a Brotherhood retreat.

I Feel

(About 30 minutes to 1 hour)

Materials: pens, index cards, a bag (or other receptacle)

Objective: Outgoing or shy, confident or insecure, all young people can feel vulnerable and therefore need encouraging feedback. This workshop allows youth to voice their communication preferences and highlights shared concerns.

1. Reflection (15–20 minutes)

Distribute a pen and four index cards to each person. (Facilitators can also participate in this activity.) Have each person complete the following statements on a separate index card. They should not write their name on the cards. When they are finished they should place their card into the paper bag.

> I feel embarrassed when . . .
> I feel smart when . . .
> I feel ignored when . . .
> I feel respected when . . .

32

2. Report Back (30 minutes)

After you have gathered everyone's card, begin reading the responses aloud. Have your co-facilitator or a youth volunteer record the responses on large paper using a different sheet for each category. Rather than repeat answers, the recorders can make a note of the number of people who gave the same or similar response.

3. Discussion (15–20 minutes)

Once your group has reviewed all of the questions, have them look for patterns and give their opinion of what the responses suggest about the group. For example:

> *What are some of our group's similarities and differences?*
> *What are some of the most important ideas we should remember when interacting with each other?*
> *Which behaviors will be easy to put into action and which will be hard, and why?*
> *How can we support each other to practice positive interactions?*

An Experience I Had That Changed Me
(1-1/2 hours or two 45-minute sessions)
Materials: pen, paper

Objective: During a break in school or program activities (e.g., winter or summer vacation), your group members may have had little or no interaction. Even if they did, it may not have been within the formal setting of your class, Advisory, or program. This is an activity for rekindling bonds through spoken and written dialogue.

1. Reflective Writing (20 minutes)
Have each person find a spot in the room where she or he can sit alone since this is a quiet activity. If space is limited, have each person sit with at least one empty chair between them and the next person. This arrangement helps everyone to focus and minimizes opportunity for conversation. Distribute a pen and paper to each person, and write the following statement on the board.

An experience I had this summer that changed me . . .

Tell your group that you are asking them to reflect on the impact of their experiences, whether great or small. To help them get started, instruct them to brainstorm a list of the activities they did during the break on the left side of their paper. On the right side, they should then write how the experience made them feel or what it meant to them.

2. Essay Writing (20 minutes)
Once your group has generated their lists, have them choose one experience that stands out for them and which they want to write about. To help them flesh out the details and impact of the experience, ask them to describe:

Where it took place
Who was involved
What were the actions that occurred
How did they feel then and why they think they remembered the experience

Give your group 5-, 2- and 1-minute warnings so they know in advance how much time they have to finish. (Everyone may not finish his or her essay and feel disappointed that time has run out. Encourage them to continue working on it and to share it with you and/ or the group at another session if they would like.)

This is a natural break if facilitating the workshop over two days.
Collect the essays at the end of the first day and begin the second day by giving your group a few minutes to review their work.

3. Read Alouds (20–30 minutes)

Ask for volunteers to read all or part of their essay. Since the objective of the activity is to re-establish ties, encourage everyone to share something, even if only a few lines. Of course, do not force anyone to share who does not want to. Facilitators should share their writing as well, though it's best to wait until most of the young people have presented.

4. Rap-up (20 minutes)

Facilitate an open discussion that allows young people to ask each other questions and discuss the concept of personal change. Questions to generate discussion are:

How do you know when you have changed?
How do you think your personal changes will impact your relationships with your friends, family, and teachers? What about with our group?

Proverbs, Folktales & Fables:
Oral Tradition from the Root to Today
(2-1/2 hours or four 45-minute sessions)
Materials: large paper and writing paper; markers and pens;
and selected proverbs, folktales, and fables (see Resources below)

Overview: Oral tradition dates back to Africa and was one of the many cultural traditions Africans brought with them when they were captured and shipped to the Americas. Those with talent in the telling of fables, folktales, and proverbs were revered for their wisdom and for being keepers of the history and ways of the community. They may have been spiritual or political leaders, or ordinary people who shouldered the responsibility for maintaining and passing down history. In many respects, the oral tradition gives power to those who do not write history books or set social norms. It allows "ordinary" folk to sit in judgment, to become lords over words, to make fun of the powerful, and to help bring order to their world. This workshop explores the roots of the oral tradition as passed down in proverbs, folktales, and fables. It introduces youth to principal characters and highlights history, beliefs and the experiences of Black people, both in the past and as reflected in contemporary Hip Hop and spoken word movements.

Preparation:

a) Choose several proverbs, folktales, and fables: a) that will resonate with your group based on their age and gender, b) that bring out the history and present realities of the oral tradition (i.e., Hip Hop), and c) that deal with such issues as education, personal responsibility, violence, peace, respecting one's elders, the role of children, and gender roles. They should also provoke discussion and reflection.

b) Choose one fable with the Anansi character and one with Brer Rabbit to introduce to youth and to provide a comparison of African and African-American fables. Identify key points and choose images to present. We suggest you create a chart with a column for each character and list of its attributes.

c) Write the proverbs on large paper and display around the room.

d) Make copies of the proverbs, folktales, and fables to distribute to your group, as well as copies of the *Young People's Proverbs* handout (page 38).

Workshop:

1. Connecting to Oral Tradition (20 minutes)

Ask your group to define "proverb", "folktale", "fable" and "oral tradition". Also have them share any proverbs, fables or folktales they heard while growing up. For example, a Brotherhood/Sister Sol Co-Founder showed his father a fable with the Shine character. His father, raised in the 1940s and 1950s in North Carolina, already knew the story by ear and responded, "Hell, I didn't know we were doing folktales. I just thought we were talking mess." Use the discussion to help your group understand that:

> Proverbs are short sayings that reveal a truth or promote a lesson.

> Folktales are part of the oral tradition of passing on traditional tales or legends, especially those that are considered to be false or superstitious.

> Fables are stories that convey a lesson or make meaningful observations about one's community, culture, or the larger society.

> Oral tradition uses the spoken word to pass on stories, lessons, and legacy. Within the United States, it stems from it being illegal for Blacks to read and write until the late 19th century. Many did risk their lives, though secretly learning how to read and write.

Now ask your group why they think some societies use the oral tradition. Have them also consider whether or not Hip Hop is an oral tradition.

2. Proverbs (30 minutes)

Have your group read the proverbs you selected, then discuss the issues and ideas each speaks to and what each means to them. They should also reflect on what the proverbs suggest about the culture where they originate. Also distribute and discuss *Young People's Proverbs*.

3. Fables & Folktales (30 minutes)

Have your group read the fables/folktales you selected, then discuss with them the characters, issues, and ideas and what each means to them. Some points to bring out are that they:

> Capture the attention of children (particularly the animated representations of the animals) who were often the target audience.

Concealed information during the time of slavery and thus protected the storyteller. For example, when Harriet Tubman was coming near, slaves would tell stories about Brer Rabbit, who was physically weak, but incredibly smart, and who constantly overcame the evil humans (slaveowners).

Enabled people to hold onto their culture and beliefs when they had been stripped of everything (as during the Middle Passage).

Helped order society in slave communities when there existed no white laws governing criminal acts (i.e., adultery, theft by one enslaved person from another). Enslaved Blacks would "put 'em on the banjo" and tell stories about the wrongdoer to ostracize him/her from the community.

Was a precursor to the Dozens (a Black American verbal banter of one-upmanship where folks talk trash back and forth), as well as to Hip Hop. (See the "Signifying Monkey" in *Afro-American Folktales* edited by Roger D. Abrahams, page 101 cited in Resources.)

4. Brer Rabbit & Anansi (30 minutes)
Have your group take turns reading the Brer Rabbit and Anansi stories aloud. After sharing their impressions of the stories, have them identify connections between the fables. Next, display the character chart you created and images you selected. Review and discuss them with your group, highlighting their observations and adding yours.

Rap-up (30 minutes)
Have your group reconsider if they heard any proverbs or folktales growing up now that they have a better sense of what these oral traditions are. Provide time for them to share. Then have them write their own proverbs and ask each person to read his/her to the group.

Young People's Proverbs

Brotherhood members, ages 13–17, Harlem and the Lower East Side, New York

Sometimes we are the pigeon, sometimes we are the statue.

Don't be slow in telling a dog that he is heading off a cliff.

A mouse can only beat a cat if it doesn't run.

If there is a wall in front of you, don't be scared to climb over it.

Family is as important as your heart.

Hard work will feed you.

Don't judge if you don't want to be judged.

You will not find true strength in your arms and legs, but in your mind and heart.

Don't point at a lion unless you want it to tear your arm off.

Do not fear what you do not understand.

If you kill, and take a brother's life, you are killing his family,
but if you save a brother's life, you are saving his family.

Don't fight unless you know what you are fighting for.

You are loving someone, but you don't know how to love.

Jumping in the pool without knowing how to swim will cause you to drown.

Why walk alone when we can walk together?

You're about to die, and you don't even know why.

You're eating cereal, but you don't even have any milk.

He who knows must teach, and he who doesn't know must think.

Do not drink beer if you do not want to get drunk.

Two who are well united can take on a whole army.

· · · · ·
RESOURCES

For Featured Workshops

Afro-American Folktales and
African Folktales
Roger D. Abrahams (Ed.)

African Proverbs
Sophia Bedford-Pierce and Wolf Leslaw (Eds.)

African Proverbs
Gerd De Ley (Ed.)

African-American Proverbs: In Context
S. W. Anand Prahiad

African Wisdom
Tokunboh Addeken

The People Could Fly:
American Black Folktales
Virginia Hamilton (Ed.)

General

Group Building & Icebreakers
Moving Beyond Icebreakers:
An Innovative Approach to Group Facilitation,
Learning, and Action
The Center for Teen Empowerment
www.teenempowerment.org

Silver Bullet, A Guide to Initiative Problems,
Adventure Games and Trust Activities
Karl Rohnke

Youth Leadership in Action: A Guide to
Cooperative Games and Group Activities Written
by and for Youth Leaders
Fortier and Project Adventure Inc.

39

2

Why Did This Happen?
Content, Perspective, Dialogue Workshop Model

One writes out of one thing only—one's own experience.
Everything depends on how relentlessly one forces from the experience the
last drop, sweet or bitter, it can possibly give.
James Baldwin

If you wrote from experience, you'd get maybe one book,
maybe three poems. Writers write from empathy.
Nikki Giovanni

James Baldwin and Nikki Giovanni offer contrasting perspectives on the source of writing inspiration. Is experience or empathy more important to developing a point of view and creative voice from which to write? Like solving the riddle of which came first, it is difficult to tease apart the relationship between the two. The more we explore and learn about what is outside ourselves, the more we learn about ourselves and are able to recognize connections we have to people who at first appear to be so very different from us. Experience and empathy enable us to understand the particular in the universal, and vice versa.

The Brotherhood/Sister Sol strives to develop in young people a knowledge of self that coalesces with others. We want them to hear other people's stories and to share their own so that they develop an expansive understanding of humanity. It is critical they be informed about and comprehend critical issues of the day and their root causes. Exposing them to new ideas and experiences challenges them to open their minds and hearts and to bond in brotherhood and sisterhood. **Setting the Tone** begins the process of promoting understanding, compassion, and trust for developing a culture of intellectual and social engagement. Facilitators are then ready to begin implementing the Workshop Model: **Content, Perspective, Dialogue** (or **CPD**).

Reflective writing links and surrounds each of **CPD**'s elements as young people actively engage with the words they read, hear, and write. (See the Venn Diagram of the model on the next page.) The written word is most obviously used to provide content and different perspectives, but is equally key to creating dialogue—through verbal exchanges, but additionally through young people's dialogue with text. During the act of writing, young people are giving critical thought to the content, perspective, and dialogue they explore. Their writing—an expression of their ideas, feelings, opinions, commitments—can take many forms (journaling, essay, poetry, spoken word, research paper), but is undertaken with purpose. Through reflective writing, young people become engaged learners able to analyze complex issues and consider their role in bringing about personal and social change.

CONTENT includes information, facts, and experiential activities a class or group acquires for engaging in informed critique and dialogue.

PERSPECTIVE is the lens through which young people critique content to examine diverse points of view and the influences from which they derive.

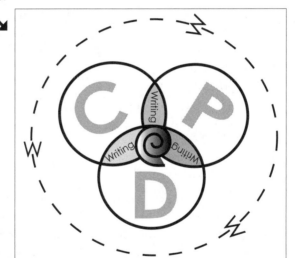

DIALOGUE brings in young people's voices in discussion and through reflective writing, and connects and illuminates content and perspective.

W refers to "writing."

ILLUSTRATION: *Elizabeth, a Lyrical Circle member, came to the brownstone one afternoon asking about women heroes. In school that day she had asked her teacher if there were any women leaders in history since all she had learned about was Betsy Ross. Her teacher explained that there were few and that most were absent from textbooks. At our brownstone a few staff members compiled a list of names and directed Elizabeth to our library and computer lab to research her question. The result of her inquiry is a poem conveying the strength of women throughout the history of the world and her obvious appreciation for those who came before. It is the ponderings of a youth seeking to understand what it means to be a woman. Elizabeth shared her poem with Bro/Sis youth and staff members and had it published in* Off the Subject: The Words of Lyrical Circle of The Brotherhood/Sister Sol. *(Read Elizabeth's poem on the next page.)*

Exploration of the issue had broader impact when Elizabeth had her poem published and she read it on a Washington, DC radio program as it offered different audiences a perspective on women leaders from a young person developing into womanhood. Through observing her ability to move others with her poetry, Elizabeth gained greater confidence in herself as a writer. She shares:

My vocabulary boasted degrading words when I walked into Bro/Sis. I cringe to hear those words now that I know the history that is attached to them. I walked into Bro/Sis unsure about whether or not I wanted to continue with higher education. I am now a sophomore at The George Washington University, considering whether or not I want a doctorate some day. When I entered the organization I was using writing as a vehicle to express the anger and frustrations that I saw in my community and dealt with daily. Bro/Sis was the first organization to give me an audience and a stage and let me know my words mattered. Writing is now not only the way I negotiate with the world, it is the way I am going to make my living.

I AM

Elizabeth Acevedo, Lyrical Circle, International Study Program (Brasil 2006)

I am the daughter of Nefertiti, born in the womb of Araminta
Manifested soul of Sojourner, blood flow of Evita
Heart of Xena, with the mind of Athena
I throw my right fist in the air,
With the other I hold my sword
Lead my people from enslavement
"Follow the drinking gourd"
Walking roads of warriors like Joan
I sit in Amazonian throne,
Crowned by Queen Hatshepsut
Lead a resistance like an Ashanti Queen against rules
Spear on my back and,
cross on my forehead
Follow Nanny of the Maroons
Fuck those who try enslave me!
I will let no one encage me
Wade in waters with a tribe of Isadshi Koseshi's
Try to follow the ways of Indira
Peaceful, serene, mind over matter
But I would shed blood before tears
I walk through archaic temples
Ancient drumbeats guide my feet
Pharaohs prophesized my coming
Wise men composed epics in my name
My story has already been told
On old pyramid walls in hieroglyphics
And by God's hand in the book of St. Peter
I dance capoera through the blows of persecutors
Their fist shall not hurt me
Real leaders never fall they merely stumble
How dare someone question who I am?
How dare anyone question my descendancy?
I am Birth Giver
I am Queen
I am Warrior
I am Woman
I am the daughter of Nefertiti born in the womb of Araminta
Manifested soul of Sojourner blood flow of Evita
Heart of Xena with the mind of Athena
Born with my right fist in the air
And a sword in my left

44

CPD is a circular learning model—Content, Perspective, and Dialogue—a kind of call and response that continually speak to each other and are interdependent. To use one or two alone will not adequately realize the model's potential. The elements are also nonlinear. You need not begin with Content and end with Dialogue, but could just as effectively start a workshop with Dialogue (such as brainstorming or reflective writing) that triggers young people's thinking and brings out their knowledge about the topic. This information can then guide you in choosing materials and activities that will enhance young people's knowledge and experiences (Content) and Perspective. Alternatively, you could begin by taking young people to a movie (Content) and then facilitate a workshop covering the movie's topic in detail. A Brotherhood chapter went to see *Hotel Rwanda*. Moved by the atrocities of the civil war the movie depicts, they wanted to learn more about the internecine conflicts in Africa and were therefore inspired to read lengthy articles and listen to a lecturette (a 15–40 minute presentation) on Darfur, Sudan, about which they had heard, but knew few specifics. Although neither Content, Perspective, nor Dialogue necessarily precedes one another, identifying curriculum issues or themes and a list of specific topics provides a roadmap for workshop planning.

> **CPD** is a circular workshop model— the elements a kind of call and response that continually speak to each other.

The Bro/Sis library with diverse literature and educational tools.

Identifying Focus Issues & Workshop Topics

The Mission Statement of The Brotherhood/Sister Sol reads:

> *The Brotherhood/Sister Sol is not simply an organization; it is more accurately a way of life. Providing young men and women with an opportunity to explore their ideas, identity, and future among peers, with the support and guidance of their immediate elders, is a natural method for promoting positive development into man/womanhood.*

> *The Brotherhood/Sister Sol has been created to address the dire need for supportive programs for Black and Latino/a youth who are surrounded by the poverty, drugs, violence, racism, and mis-education that plague America's cities. The Brotherhood/Sister Sol provides these youth with the knowledge, resources, opportunity, and love necessary in order to understand and overcome these negative pressures, as well as the skills to combat them.*

This statement summarizes the context and guiding vision of our work, and is from which we identified the *10 Curriculum Focus Issues*. These are the issues our members (Black and Latino/a youth) confront ("poverty, drugs, violence, racism, and mis-education") and what they need to "understand and overcome." BHSS believes it is crucial that our members:

Objective	Focus Issue(s)
Study their history, culture, and experiences	**1**: *Pan African & Latino/a History*
Learn the root cause of and strategies for dealing with oppression and violence	**2**: *Sexism & Misogyny* **3**: *Conflict Resolution & Bias Reduction* **4**: *Political Education & Social Justice*
Learn how to take care of their holistic needs and avoid negative temptations	**5**: *Mind, Body & Spirit* **6**: *Drugs & Substance Abuse* **7**: *Sexual Education & Responsibility*
Develop a range of skills and capacities and a strong sense of self	**8**: *Leadership Development* **9**: *Educational Achievement*
Work collectively to counteract the destructive conditions they face	**10**: *Community Service & Responsibility*

Schools, classrooms, and community organizations can reference their own mission statements toward identifying curriculum focus issues or themes. Teachers and youth workers might also have their class or group develop a mission statement (similar to what Brotherhood and Sister Sol chapters do) to help bring out common interests and concerns. The number of issues is unimportant. However, the curriculum issues or themes should:

Connect to the mission or objectives of your class, group, or program.
Be broad enough to allow you to cover a range of topics.
Be relevant to your youth.
Offer youth an opportunity to contribute their knowledge and viewpoints.
Highlight individual and universal perspectives, enabling youth to connect
    personal experiences to communal issues.
Generate ideas for materials and activities to bring out the issues/themes.

Informed by our *10 Curriculum Focus Issues* we choose workshop topics our members have expressed an interest in and/or ones we think are important for them to explore. They have enjoyed learning about youth leaders (e.g., the role of youth in the anti-apartheid movement), gender roles and expectations (e.g., images of women in Hip Hop), and current social events they experience and/or confront (e.g., police brutality, hate crimes, military recruitment). Questions that can help you choose a workshop topic are:

How does it relate to your broad focus issues or theme?
How does it reflect the interests and experiences of your youth?
How does it highlight young people's ethnicity, culture, gender, class,
    or sexual orientation?
How will it deepen their knowledge of self and humanity?
How will it support development of young people's leadership and critical
    thinking skills?
How will it support group building?

A workshop topic can speak to multiple issues and objectives. As an example, a workshop on the image of women in Hip Hop could cover three of our *10 Curriculum Focus Issues*:

Sexism & Misogyny: The group views a series of videos featuring scantily clad women doing sexually explicit dance moves, and compare it to the imagery and actions of men in the videos.

Pan African & Latino/a History: The group learns about the history of Hip Hop and its emergence in the South Bronx, then examines how the genre has evolved as a result of moving away from its roots.

Leadership Development: The group creates a video challenging the negative portrayal of women and presents it to peers as an educational or organizing strategy. Using video as their format demonstrates their respect for the form while critiquing specific content.

At times we choose a topic that is of interest to our members, but it is difficult for them to take in. When this happens we encourage them to not turn away from that which is painful, but to acknowledge their feelings as an essential part of the learning process. Exploring topics that potentially evoke strong feelings requires having worked on **Setting the Tone** and creating a learning environment in which young people can honestly and safely express anger, sadness, and pain.

FROM MISSION STATEMENT TO WORKSHOP TOPIC

A ***Mission Statement*** summarizes the collective values, intentions, and characteristics of a group or class, program, organization, or school.

Focus Issues derive from the Mission Statement. They are the overarching class, program, organization, or school themes.

Workshop Topics derive from Focus Issues. They provide specific content for the learning and reflection activities.

ILLUSTRATION: *A Brotherhood chapter had a session on the state of Black men. They read two articles that detailed issues facing Black men in urban America. The articles focused on issues related to prison, lack of educational achievement, violence, and voting. After a two-hour session that utilized quotes of reflection, statistics, a close reading of the articles out loud (stopping on unfamiliar words and focusing on major points made by the author), and conversation based on the young men's personal experiences, the chapter was asked to free write for 20 minutes. Their Chapter Leaders were careful to include in the conversation that the reason for sharing this information was not to leave a room of 16- and 17-year-old young men depressed or disillusioned, but instead to provide information, to help share experiences that would ultimately help everyone feel empowered. By knowing the realities, they were told, they would also learn the obstacles that must be overcome. By knowing how pervasive the struggles are, they would learn there is nothing wrong with them personally and therefore should not internalize the poverty, mis-education, and racism they face, but instead understand that these conditions are systemic. The young brothers realized they are not alone and that, once informed and with their Chapter Leaders' support and guidance, they were expected to overcome the realities they learned about. While their writings reflect anger and pain, they also convey a resolute desire to achieve and change their realities.*
(Read "Reflections on the State of Black Men" on pages 50–52. Sequan, whose piece you will see, developed his work into a college essay, going on to earn a full scholarship to Brandeis University after considering dropping out of high school to get a General Equivalency Diploma.)

REFLECTIONS ON THE STATE OF BLACK MEN

Intrinsic Kings Brotherhood Chapter

Today was a good session. I always learn a lot when I come, and today was like any other time. Brotherhood points out facts and articles that don't really catch everyone's eyes…. The conversations we have are great. Khary explains situations and breaks down facts and statistics to where people can understand them. I'm glad that I joined Brotherhood because I don't know what I would be doing if I didn't. I love the aura that is the brownstone, it's the kind of aura that is loving and learning.

Most teenage boys don't have an organization to go to where everything is positive, and I'm glad that I do. Some children I know ask me why I keep going to The Brotherhood and I always say, "Why not?" It's a positive place to go, and my home is not always positive and for me the streets are never positive, so why not go to a positive place? **Renaldo Edwards**

Living as a young black man in this world is a very strong hardship to deal with. It's crazy how people try and cover up racism. It's basically a conspiracy to eliminate every black and brown person. They bring us here against our will and then they try and get rid of us.

I am also thinking about how so many people do not truly open their eyes and see the truth about the world. I am tired of people keeping the hidden truth away from us. I am tired of everything bad that happens, happening to us: AIDS, incarceration, police brutality, stereotypes, etc.

Now I'm thinking about different ways to get out of this situation. I don't just want myself to get out, I want others to get out. I know that this will not completely stop, but if I can help, then why not? The first step to helping is to get myself out of the situation. So, one day I will be a neurosurgeon, not just for the money, but for the respect I will get. I want to show that a young black man, coming from Harlem, with basically nothing, can get out of this alive, and happy. I want to show that black men are not mentally inferior.

I will go to college and learn from others, however, I know that I have to reach the truth for myself. My life will not depend on others. I will also give back and I'll try my best to help out as much as I can. Knowing that I have the support of my brothers I can really do anything I set my mind to. **Garry Baez**

The idea of being seen and treated as an equal dwells in my mind. Police brutality is a reality I never wanted to accept because I aspired to become an officer. I can no longer close my eyes and pretend nothing has happened because racism still plagues our justice system and the first initiative I must take to improve the system is to acknowledge the problem. Though my fellow members, brothers and chapter leaders' anecdotes I have seen the atrocities that drain the spirit of the young black male. Random stops by the police and an abuse of their power has scarred many and weakened others. I do not understand why we as black males and black people should fear those who vowed to protect us. Justice cannot be allowed to wander around blindfolded in black communities violating people's personal space and state of being.

The lesson I have learned today does not hinder me but instead prepares me for what is to come. A white man leaves his son riches in a novel, but a black male leaves his son with a torn mother, police who target him for simply being black and a lacking of knowledge of self. I feel as though the world has used color and material possessions to define an individual—the idea is that most accept this, and that is why there is no change.

Many argue that capitalism is all about moving up in the world, but understand how few become millionaires and billionaires. Also, consider how this race started and all the obstacles and devious traps that have been implemented to place the black and Hispanic communities behind the starting line. People speak as though slavery was not a crime to humanity, when in actually it was constructed to destroy the beams of our humanity and drive. We cannot assume that we all started on the same level and had one common goal. **Sequan Born Spigner**

51

Sequan went on to develop his first reflections into the college essay below.

When I walk out of my house each day I cannot help but feel I am in a battlefield. Missiles are flying over my head and carnivorous bullets originating from advertisements and stereotypes are harming anyone with traces of individuality. My only weapons are my words, ideas, and thirst for knowledge. I have been born not only to win the battle, but also the war. I do this while focusing on the words of Frederick Douglass as if they were the solution to all that is wrong: "Without struggle there is no progress." I will struggle to succeed.

I have realized the atrocities of today with the help of The Brotherhood/Sister Sol (Bro/Sis), a non-profit organization stationed in Harlem, NY, created to empower Black and Latino youth. I am not what the mass media projects to the world, but instead I am human. I am an individual, not a statistic or consumer as viewed by the corporations of the world. Even though I am commonly portrayed as a hustler, gangster, rapper, thief, and misogynistic jester by the media and throughout history, I live in a reality where I am a brother, son, leader, and young man with goals that will shake the world itself. I have accepted that my brown skin is inescapable and I am proud of it and of my history.

Throughout my life, I have faced an endless amount of hardships. Born into a single-parent household setting, my mother had to provide for the two of us, and many of her own problems were taken out on me. The biggest change came in my junior year when my living environment transformed from a safe haven to a place I detested; my mother continuously dealt with abusive men and too often forgot she had a 16-year-old son. The pain from being put aside, as though I was a toy no longer desired by its owner, took a toll on my motivation. During my junior year I had to take a leave of absence due to family stress. By November my mother decided to move down south to a place where I knew no one. Three weeks later I was back in New York City. This led to an excessive amount of absences that, though excused, created a difficult environment. The experience was disabling, preventing me from learning and participating to the fullest of my abilities while leaving me vulnerable to the razor-sharp questioning of my peers. I was embarrassed by my situation and unable to fully interact with most peers, except for the members of Bro/Sis.

The Brotherhood, a section of Bro/Sis, is a rites of passage program for Black and Latino males where we learn what it means to be men, brothers, and leaders. The Brotherhood is split into chapters. The chapter I belong to is called The Intrinsic Kings and is composed of fourteen males from my high school. They are my support network, refueling the engine of my heart's motivation. I moved out of my mother's house in November of 2006. The stress of having to provide for myself was exhausting and made me consider pursuing a General Equivalency Diploma. Luckily, my brothers would not allow it, and said, "You have too much potential." With these strong, positive people all around me there is no way I can ever fall and not have the strength to regain balance.

I see life as an obstacle course now. I will face challenges, but I can look back on what I have overcome and be ready for anything. Like Tupac Shakur, "I am the rose that grew from concrete" to become a poet who uses his words to influence the minds of the world today. Despite my mistakes, hardships, and struggles to blossom into the person I am now, I do not see myself as a victim. I am the victor because I still stand strong.

·····

STRATEGIES for Implementing
Content, Perspective, Dialogue

1. Choose socially salient, diverse and challenging content.

BHSS has assembled a library that is a resource for our members and staff. Workshop content comes from novels, articles, poems, statistics, maps, music videos, blogs, documentaries, popular film, art exhibits, plays, and guest speakers. We select resources our members may not normally read because they are unfamiliar with it or think it will be uninteresting or too difficult to understand. Content that is too easy, dense, or long will be boring. Though we occasionally read entire novels or memoirs with our members, we break them down into sections of about 25–30 pages, a length we think they will have time to read over a week and not interfere with their homework assignments, jobs, or household chores. Depending on the density of the text and a group's reading ability, we choose excerpts or articles that range from one to eight pages long (or about 500–3000 words).

Look for resources that offer complexity, forcing young people to think deeply and learn new vocabulary and concepts. It will give them a sense of accomplishment and pride when they grasp difficult content. It is important for facilitators to read all material in advance in **53** order to anticipate young people's questions about the meaning of words or specific facts. This may require some basic research, enough to provide background information that hopefully sparks their group's interest in doing further exploration.

Some young people will grapple with material that others find easy. The objective is to raise the bar for everyone, being sensitive to not embarrass a young person, but encouraging everyone to try reading a passage, to sound out words or foreign names, and to voice their ideas however unformed. By perpetually practicing rituals established during **Setting the Tone**, youth become increasingly supportive of each other, trusting they will receive the same respect.

SOURCES FOR READING CONTENT
Newspaper articles and
    OpEd columns
Magazine articles and editorials
Selections from anthologies of
    essays and short stories
Memoir excerpts
Statistical data (for example):
    Children's Defense Fund
    Department of Education
    U.S. Census

Workshop content should offer young people alternative perspectives. A workshop on a current event might include articles on the topic from the *New York Daily News* (or other tabloid), *The New York Times*, *Amsterdam News* (a weekly Black newspaper), and *Alternet* (an online news source). A workshop on immigration and its impact on urban areas could include perspectives from a local business owner, a successful immigrant college student, and a family who employs undocumented workers. Providing young people with multiple perspectives helps broaden their awareness and sharpen their reasoning. Their opinions develop out of hearing viewpoints that are both similar to and different from their own.

> Providing young people with multiple perspectives helps broaden their awareness and sharpen their reasoning.
> What is most important is that they are interested in content. It must seem relevant to them.

What is clearly most important is that young people are interested in the content. It must seem relevant to them. They appreciate reading material by and about people "like them," characters or people of the same gender, ethnicity, class, or sexuality who are confronted by similar social issues (urban life, cliques, family drama, romantic relationships, gangs, the war, sexual experiences, racism, sexism, injustice). We use personal stories (including from youth, staff, and guest speakers) to highlight the unique and collective history and culture of Black and Latino men and women. These stories convey that despite great suffering throughout time and the endurance of racism, sexism, and other forms of oppression, Black and Latino/a people come from a long line of tradition, achievement leadership, and strength. Stories also serve to deepen connections between diverse people.

ILLUSTRATION: *We facilitate a workshop entitled* Echoing Baldwin & Torres *using* Letter to My Nephew on the One Hundredth Anniversary of the Emancipation *(James Baldwin) and* Letter to A Son Like Me *(Edwin Torres). After reading and discussing the essays, the workshop ends with our members writing a letter to their future sons and daughters. Baldwin's essay written 50 years ago has resonance with our members because it takes place in a Harlem that is not so different from today and involves a Black boy becoming a man while dealing with racism and violence, as do our members. Torres's essay is a contemporary piece that speaks to the immigrant experience of a Latino and the challenges of navigating two cultures, as many of our members also do. Of additional significance, during this workshop we provide our members with a short biography of the writers. Baldwin's personal story naturally incorporates into the lesson the experiences of a Black gay male who struggled throughout his life to find peace in a country that continually sought to deny his worth, despite his central place in America's literary pantheon. When Baldwin's bio is shared at the end of the workshop, the fact of his sexuality, in particular, often becomes less a point of criticism than might otherwise have been because now our members have connected to his life as a Black man from Harlem with a high school education, forcing them to reassess any feelings of homophobia.* (Details about this workshop can be found in *Brother, Sister, Leader: The Official Curriculum of The Brotherhood/Sister Sol.* Read two members' "A Letter to My Son" on page 56.)

Finally, some content is chosen not because it appeals to young people interests, but because it provides important background information or description, as well as exposure to diverse stories and experiences. Statistics, maps, graphs, photographs, and short excerpts from encyclopedias are useful, as are materials that are easy-to-read and not overly detailed.

A LETTER TO MY SON
Invincible/Untouchable Chapter

My Boy,

I shouldn't address you as a boy anymore. A boy is someone who walks around and lives his life innocent and blind to his surroundings. A boy is someone who is still preparing to accept the world he is about to enter. You are far from a boy. I am writing this letter to you because as part of leaving that phase of boyhood, I want you to understand and grip certain ideas that will help you cope and succeed in this world. One of the greatest (if not the greatest) virtues you could ever own and use is Love. Love for yourself, love for your family and love for everybody. Love is an essential tool for survival in the world we live in because there is so much hate and fear. No matter what anyone tells you, love is the only way to fight hate and fear. What is hate? The hate I want you to see is the hate the world has for you simply because you are of color. In America, your life is foretold by white people. The hate I wanted you to see and avoid is the ignorance and fear that plagues America today. What is fear? Fear is hate. The most honest thing I can say to you is that this country wasn't built for you to succeed. This country is filled with lost Black and Latino men. They're lost because they have to fit the mold of how this country wants you to be. This country was built for you to be comfortable where you are and to never progress.

You are about to enter a world where everything is supposed to be against you and there is nothing to help you. The entire world is wrong. You have love. And with love, you can and will defy the odds. **Jose Lora**

• • •

First off, son, I hope you know I love you and I will always be there for you. You are 12 now and things are gonna change. Everything you are about to go through, I have been through.

Never be afraid of change. Embrace it, use it, but don't fear it.

Never stop loving yourself and who you are. There are too many that have lost themselves.

Always be a man. A man is not the guy selling drugs on the street or the man who never cries or shows feelings. A man shows love, speaks truth, is trustworthy and stands up for the rights of others.

I can't tell you how to live your life because the best way to learn is by experience. But heed what I have written. Understand these are my truths and you must come to know your own. **Kendall Calyen**

2. Expose young people to extraordinary and diverse learning experiences.

Exposure to new and firsthand experiences lets young people see for themselves and take safe risks. Opportunities for experiential learning, especially in cities, abound. Many are free or inexpensive. We take advantage of New York City's vast cultural offerings such as museums, galleries, plays, and performances. We also conduct wilderness retreats, college tours, and study programs in Africa and Latin America. These are, of course, costly, though extremely worthwhile activities for which groups can fundraise. Whether local, regional, or global, firsthand experiences increase self-confidence and foster cross-cultural competence.

ILLUSTRATION: *A Sister Sol chapter attended school just a few blocks from a street lined with Indian restaurants. The street might as well have been in India, so foreign was it to the young women. Knowing this, the Chapter Leaders took them on a dinner outing. The restaurant's moody lighting, embroidered tapestries, Indian music, and Tandoori oven was designed to transport you to India. The chapter was impressed, less by the food that they gamely tried, than by it being a "romantic" and "fancy" place. These young sisters had regularly referred to all Asian people as Chinese, so the Chapter Leaders also used the setting to give an informal geography and cultural lesson about Asia, and raised for discussion the cliché that people of similar ethnicity look alike. It was an outing the chapter would fondly recall, and one that expanded their neighborhood and cultural awareness.*

EMPATHY, EXPERIENCE & WRITING

Challenging content and experiences:

> Provide young people with topics and information.

> Expand their knowledge of self and the world, helping them to make connections between diverse experiences and deepen their understanding and analysis of the human condition.

> Add specificity and clarity to their ideas and opinions so that they accurately convey information and meaning.

> Increase their self-confidence, which translates to greater risk taking with their writing and sharing it publicly.

Keep activities intriguing. Young people often end up enjoying activities they perceive will be boring. Sister Sol members were taken to see *Real Women Have Curves*, a movie including English, Spanish, and subtitles. Though initially disappointed that it had subtitles, they ended up really enjoying it and had much to say about its message. Their Chapter Leaders knew *Real Curves* would be appealing because it is a coming-of-age story about a strong, young Latina dealing with feelings about her body, awakening sexuality, and personal dreams while straddling Mexican and American culture. Many young women confront these same issues. When youth have too much information about a workshop or outing in advance, they can make negative assumptions about its appeal. We therefore do not always share activity specifics, a strategy our members are now very familiar with. They try, with little avail, to get their Chapter Leaders to tell them where the group is going. When parental consent is required, we provide general information such as the outing is to a movie, play, or exhibit, but not the details.

You might take a tour of young people's neighborhood, or another area of the city. Ask them to closely observe that which they see every day, or which is different from or similar to their community. How are residents interacting with each other? How maintained is the neighborhood? What spaces are available for young people? Discuss and have them write about their observations. During a museum tour, let your group walk through the exhibit at its own pace, however quickly, though be nearby to answer their questions or listen to their impressions. Have youth keep a list of questions they have about the exhibit or identify a piece of art or information they are drawn to. When the group meets up to discuss the exhibit, they can ask their questions and describe in detail the object/display they chose and why.

When going on outings, ask young people to remove their iPods and to not text on their cellphones so they can pay attention to their surroundings. If the outing is to a park or is a retreat outside of the city, encourage young people to listen to the sounds of the wilderness, to observe the foliage and sky. This will lure them into the natural environment and also take their attention away from less appealing elements (e.g., the weather, length of the hike, bugs).

Take young people out of their comfort zone. There are many ways to challenge young people's minds, bodies, and spirits. For some, it can be as simple as pushing them to read aloud or share their writing during a workshop. For many others, it is taking them out of their social clique or into an environment in which they might not normally venture. During workshops, we partner our members with young people with whom they have limited interaction. Using New York City as a teaching landscape, we take them around their neighborhood, and to cultural sites (e.g., Lincoln Center, galleries, Broadway plays), parks, gardens, and restaurants. We also take young people on wilderness retreats where they face such fears as bugs or the dark, and test their limits on a rock-climbing wall or ropes course. Each person's comfort zone is different, but pushing beyond it teaches important life lessons. Reaching the mountain's crest, as our members have written, becomes a metaphor for achieving success in school as a result of studying hard. With creativity, facilitating activities that challenge young people, while fostering trust building and collaboration, can take place in any open space, such as a park or gym. Create an obstacle course with chairs, boxes, or sports equipment. Have youth work in pairs, blindfolding one person who receives directions from the sighted partner to safely navigate the course. Having set the tone, young people will no doubt be each others' cheerleaders during individual and group challenges. (See Resources on page 39.)

A Dialogue circle

3. Develop good questions.

Good questions invigorate Content, Perspective and Dialogue. They reveal more than facts or right and wrong answers. Questions also have different objectives.

Open-ended Questions elicit impressions, gather general perspectives, and promote critical reflection and analysis, for example:

> What are your (thoughts, comments, feelings) about what you just (heard, learned, read, experienced)?
> How does the topic connect to your personal experiences?
> What do you think the writer is trying to convey, and why?

Focusing Questions probe for specific information or ideas, and assess comprehension of the topic, for example:

> What are the main points of this (article, story, essay)?
> What role does (a character) play in the story?
> What is the problem being described and who does it affect?

Clarification Questions are explanatory and ensure understanding, for example:

> What do you mean by that?
> Can you give me an example of what you are saying?
> Are you saying (fill in your summary of their comment)?

Practice the concept that "no question or idea is stupid." Make sure each young person has her or his say. Record everyone's idea when notating responses on the board. Coax the participation of each young person.

Regardless of the type of question, it is important to model consideration of all perspectives by practicing the concept that "no question or idea is stupid." Make sure each young person has their say, and record everyone's idea when notating responses on the board. During some discussions it may be particularly important to have everyone contribute to the dialogue. To coax participation, inform your group at the start that everyone will be asked to share; then either go around the circle or take answers one-by-one until everyone has spoken. Do not rush this process, but allow young people to respond at their own pace. You may need to return to a young person if she is still gathering her thoughts, but encourage her to offer something, however brief. To reinforce the essentialness of young people's participation, thank them for their comment, for sharing an intimate thought and/or and for contributing to the discussion.

Our *Framework for Analysis* offers a template for identifying the larger questions a workshop might address across six concepts:

1: Knowledge of Self
2: Knowledge of the World
3: Unity & Community
4: Leadership
5: Power
6: Transformation & Liberation

Using James Baldwin's *Letter to My Nephew* we highlight short excerpts to demonstrate the kinds of questions a facilitator can ask to help young people explore the essay through the Framework's six concepts (see pages 62–63). A workshop does not have to address each of the concepts, or in order, but it should be designed to help young people make personal and universal connections to the content toward finding, expressing, and using their voices around issues that matter to them.

1. Knowledge of Self

An understanding of our beliefs, values, needs, aspirations, experiences, history, etc.

Where do I fit in?

How/why does the issue affect me?

How do I incorporate my understanding of the issue into my knowledge of self?

Baldwin Excerpt: *Like him, you are tough, dark, vulnerable, moody—with a very definite tendency to sound truculent because you want no one to think you are soft. . . . You can be destroyed by believing that you really are what the white world calls a nigger. I tell you this because I love you, and please don't ever forget it.*

Questions: *Who does Baldwin's nephew remind you of? Who can relate to the feelings or experiences Baldwin is describing?*

2. Knowledge of the World

Awareness of the world's historical, social, political, and cultural structures and issues

What are the patterns, connections, commonalities, and differences of the world's diverse structures and issues?

Baldwin Excerpt: *Now, my dear namesake, these innocent and well-meaning people, your countrymen, have caused you be born under conditions not very far removed from those described to us by Charles Dickens.*

Questions: *Why would Baldwin refer to Charles Dickens? What does London of the 1800s have to do with Harlem and the Black experience in the 1960s and the 2000s?*
(Briefly explain that Dickens wrote novels about the wretched, inhumane conditions of many Londoners in the late 1800s.)

3. Unity & Community

A perception of humanity that recognizes the world's diversity and the intrinsic links among humankind

How do local and global communities promote such concepts as individualism, apathy, unity, community, and the like?

How do they act in ways that recognize that we share one world?

Baldwin Excerpt: *There is no reason for you to try to become like white people and there is no basis whatever for their impertinent assumption that they must accept you. . . . You must accept them and accept them with love. For these innocent people have no other hope. They are, in effect, still trapped in a history which they do not understand. . . .*

Questions: *What do you think Baldwin means by "innocent"? How do you think whites might be "trapped in history"? After describing his own experiences with racism, why would Baldwin say that Blacks need to accept whites with love?*

4. Leadership

A sense of personal or collective empowerment to take charge or action

How is leadership being manifested?

Who is the leader attracting to his/her cause, and why?

How is the leader motivating?

Baldwin Excerpt: *I said that it was intended that you should perish in the ghetto. . . . You have, and many of us have, defeated this intention. . . .and if the word integration means anything, this is what it means: that we, with love, shall force our brothers to see themselves as they are, to cease fleeing reality and to begin to change it.*

Questions: *What qualities do you think Baldwin believes a leader should have? How can someone move from feeling oppressed to feeling empowered?*

---

5. Power

The personal or collective ability to influence and/or exert control over others

Who has the power?

What are their resources?

How are they able to influence others and/or exert control?

Baldwin Excerpt: *I know what the world has done to my brother and how narrowly he has survived it. And I know, which is much worse, and this is the crime of which I accuse my country and my countrymen, and for which neither I nor time nor history will ever forgive them, that they destroyed and are destroying hundreds of lives and do not know it and do not want to know it.*

Questions: *What is the "crime" Baldwin is describing? What crime could be worse than racism itself? How have some people in this country been able to continually destroy the lives of others and not know it?*

---

6. Transformation & Liberation

The sense of freedom to pursue your dreams and goals regardless of your ethnicity/race, gender, class, sexuality, or other obstacles

What understandings and actions will transform individuals and communities?

How does personal transformation work toward bringing about universal liberation?

Baldwin Excerpt: *It will be hard, James, but you come from sturdy, peasant stock, men who picked cotton and dammed rivers and built railroads, and in the teeth of the most terrifying odds, achieved an unassailable and monumental dignity. You come from a long line of great poets, some of the greatest poets since Homer. One of them said, the very time I thought I was lost, My dungeon shook and my chains fell off. . . .*

Questions: *What ideas and feelings is Baldwin trying to leave his nephew with at the end of his essay? What does he want him to take away from learning about the many struggles Baldwin and other Black people have faced? Why do you think Baldwin refers to Homer? What does Homer represent?*
(Briefly describe Homer and his significance as a poet.)

WORKSHOPS

Overview: Similar to the types of critical questions described on pages 60 and 61, the workshops in this chapter offer different levels of writing. The first is open-ended and primarily a creative exercise, while the others are dependent on content. Of these, one is a collaborative group activity in which young people practice interview and planning skills, and the other introduces them to historical information through which they examine and deconstruct contemporary media. The workshops in this chapter are:

o Word Riff
o Oríkí
o Bamboozled: The History of Minstrelsy

A Bro/Sis member adding his ideas to workshop Dialogue.

Word Riff

(1-1/2–2 hours or two 45-minute sessions)

Materials: writing paper, pens, dictionary (English and/or other languages), thesaurus

Overview: Good writing pays close attention to word usage, to how their meaning and rhythm combine into expressive prose. This workshop is a fun way to have young people play around with words in a freewrite process.

1. Choose a Word (10 minutes)

Distribute pens and paper. Have each young person think of or search for a word (using the resources you gathered). They might be attracted to its meaning or the way it sounds, or it may evoke a particular memory or feeling. After everyone has selected their word, have them take a seat at least one chair away from each other, if not farther apart, in order to help them focus on their writing.

2. Riff (20–25 minutes)

Tell your group that they are to use their word in a poem, story, or essay. They can use it as frequently or as little as they like, and they can write about whatever they want. Give them 10-, 5-, and 2- minute warnings so they know in advance how much time they have to finish. (Everyone may not finish his or her essay and feel disappointed that time has run out. Encourage them to continue working on it and to share it with you and/or the group at another session if they would like.)

3. Recitation (30–45 minutes)

Have everyone read all or part of their piece.

Rap-up (15 minutes)

Have a general discussion about the assignment, providing an opportunity for them to ask each other questions and elicit their thoughts about the activity including:

> Which essays they particularly liked and why.
> What they learned from the pieces about each other's interests, writing styles or skills, etc.
> What they learned about the significance of one word.

Oríkí

(5–6 hours or about six 45-minute sessions)
Materials: writing paper, pens, guest speaker

Overview: Oríkí is a West African storytelling tradition mainly practiced by women. We have adapted it into a method for introducing young people to elders in their community and professionals from different fields whom we invite to share their stories and pass down history. We also use Oríkí to help our members learn more about their program facilitators whose lives they are curious about. Young people essentially want to know how elders became who they are: *What were their struggles and setbacks? How did they overcome obstacles? Who or what helped them along the way?* Oríkí allows youth to learn lessons from those who have come before, and the experience can be especially meaningful to them when they generate the interview questions.

Preparation (2–3 hours or four 45-minute sessions):
Have your group brainstorm whom they would like to invite to their Oríkí. They should think about what they want to learn from an elder and whom they can feasibly get to participate. Thinking about local leaders, favorite authors or artists, or doing a Google search will help your group generate ideas. Making the final selection should ideally be done through consensus so that everyone can look forward to the visit. After choosing the speaker, divide your group or have them volunteer for one of three tasks:

1) Inviting and prepping the speaker—They will get contact information, develop a letter of invitation, and make follow-up phone calls to set the date, give the location, provide the speaker with the Oríkí questions, and describe the workshop's format.

2) Developing Oríkí questions and interviewing the speaker—They will compile a list of questions to submit to the speaker in advance, as well as conduct the interview during the workshop.

3) Creating a biography of the speaker and introducing him/her during the workshop—They will research and compile information about the speaker, including related materials (e.g., organization brochures, books, artwork, etc.), and present it during Oríkí.

Provide time for the groups to update each other since it will be important that they exchange information. For example, having the speaker's biographical information will inform the development of Oríkí questions. The groups can also give each other suggestions.

Workshop:

1. Oríkí (about 1 hour, or if necessary a 45-minute session)

After arranging chairs in a circle, have Group 3 introduce the Oríkí speaker and display the materials they gathered. Group 2 then conducts its interview. Facilitators should close the Oríkí with a Q & A and general discussion.

2. Reflective Writing & Sharing (30 minutes to 1 hour)

Following the Oríkí, have your group do reflective writing: What did they learn from the guest, and did her or his story influence them in any way? Ask for volunteers to share all or part of their writing. (Make sure your group sends a thank-you note to its guest.)

NOTE: We incorporate the spirit of Oríkí into most of our workshops by providing a brief biography of authors, historical figures, or leaders whose work our members are reading or whose lives they are learning about.

Bamboozled: The History of Minstrels

(3-1/2–4 hours or four to five 45-minute sessions)
Materials: *Bamboozled*, a film by Spike Lee (DVD or video), TV/VCR/DVD,
Overview of Minstrel History & Characters HANDOUT (pages 70–73)

Overview: This workshop developed from our members' interest in seeing Spike Lee's movie, *Bamboozled*. Having been part of our organization for several years, they rightly assumed their Chapter Leaders would want to take them to the movie, and they also knew it would be as much an educational experience as entertainment. *Bamboozled* explores the representation of Blacks in Hollywood, posing the provocative question: how far have they really come from the early days? This workshop provides participants with a context for understanding *Bamboozled* and an opportunity to analyze the film and the position of Black entertainers in mainstream America, yesterday and today. The workshop can be conducted over two sessions with one being for viewing and taking notes on the film and the other for facilitating a follow-up discussion.

1. Minstrelsy (45–60 minutes)

Have your group read and discuss the *Overview of Minstrel History & Characters* HANDOUT. Use the following questions to help them explore the impact of minstrelsy on contemporary Black Hollywood:

> Who do they think makes the real money in the entertainment industry (e.g., actors, writers, directors, studios)?

> Why do they think that, overwhelmingly, the majority of Black TV programs are comedies? And why are they mostly relegated to a few stations?

> Thinking about comedic figures as well as "gangsta" rap characters, how are Black people represented in TV and film? What do these images say about how they are perceived?

2. View *Bamboozled* (1 hour, 46 minutes or two to three 45-minute sessions)

Rap-up (30–45 minutes)

After viewing the movie, pose the following questions to your group for them to write about. Provide time for both writing and having volunteers share their ideas.

Which of the historic minstrel characters do "Manray" and "Womack" embody? Who/what do the other characters in the film represent?

What message(s) do you think Spike Lee was trying to convey, and why?

Thinking about Hattie McDaniel's statement that she would rather make $7,000 a week playing a maid, than be a maid making $7 a week, how much should performers of color compromise their integrity in order to work? What is their responsibility as actors of color to represent positive, realistic figures of people of color in film/TV? Also discuss the lack of power Blacks, Latinos, and other groups have to control their own images in the entertainment industry. Who makes decisions about what movies or music gets produced, and what are their priorities?

Overview of Minstrel History & Characters

Vaudeville* actor Thomas Dartmouth Rice is recognized as the first renowned minstrel performer. In 1828, this white man wore **Blackface**** and portrayed a stereotypical characterization of Black people: shiftless, lazy, sneaky, simple, and easily scared. The characterization was of a Black man as buffoon, as childlike, and as needing supervision. Rice's performance was of such success he decided to create a permanent name for his character. He chose Jim Crow. The name Jim was often used as a generic name for any Black man, and crows were often used to represent Black people because crows are black, seen as being sinister, and are scavengers.

> * Vaudeville was a popular form of entertainment in the early 1800s through the 1930s; a variety theatre show consisting of separate skits. ** Blackface is created by applying a concoction of burnt cork to the face, making it jet back in color. The lips are then painted bright white and greatly exaggerated in size.

Nearly a century later when the laws were written to keep the races separate, the laws were called **Jim Crow Laws**. The thought was that white society needed these laws to keep Jim Crow–type traits out of good, genteel, white society because with race mixing only the worst possible results could occur. Race mixing was defined as Black men with white women, as white men had been "mixing" with Black women in mass numbers since the first slave ships arrived from Africa (and also on the ships). Black woman were sexualized, raped, and pursued by white men. Roughly 80% of the 25 million Black people in America have substantial numbers of white ancestors.

• • •

There have been minstrel-type performers since the beginnings of slavery, with slaveowners having their slaves perform and entertain their families and the general public. These events were advertised, tickets were sold, and slaveowners made the money, of course. There were cases of prodigies, performers with no training who were master singers, pianists, and musicians. There was also a history of "low brow" performance. Slaves were made to entertain, to "shuck and jive" and be a source of amusement for slaveowners by playing music, dancing, and tapping. These forms of entertainment were the first true elements of minstrelsy.

During the 1830s and 1840s, minstrel shows exploded and were very popular until the 1930s and the dawn of the TV age. During the early years of minstrelsy most of the performers wearing Blackface where white. By the 1870s and 1880s the number of Black performers wearing Blackface grew tremendously. Many more "characters" were created that endure today, though not all used Blackface. Some of the most popular characters and figures were:

Jim Crow: lazy, sneaky, simple minded, shiftless, easily scared. He is dim-witted and always seems to mess a situation up and make a fool of himself.

Sambo: a buffoon and comic jester who wears bright, mismatched garish clothes and a permanent smile. He is always shucking and jiving and entertaining. He is usually very skinny and wears either very tight clothes or loose clothes that comically accentuate his appearance. He often talks in a rhythmic or flashy manner. He is never serious and gets through life with comedy.

Aunt Jemima: a big, fat, dark, sassy "big momma" who takes care of the white household and is not a sexual threat to the white woman of the household. She is fiercely loyal, will weep for the family, die for the family, and considers them good and Godly folk.

Uncle Ben: similar to Aunt Jemima, he could be her husband or brother. He is a cook or servant, completely loyal and very aware of social graces. He is old and has been with the family forever. He is too old to be any sexual or physical threat.

Uncle Tom: old and loyal, like Aunt Jemima and Uncle Ben. He is often a field slave or might be a coachman. He keeps other slaves in line with "old wisdom" to honor the owners and reinforce the notion that whites are good people. He is a somewhat respected elder of the slaves, but not too smart. The owners "take care of him" in a paternalistic manner. He can be counted on to be loyal till death. He is smiling, jovial, and fun loving.

Jezebel: young, "beautiful," and with a hunger for sex that cannot be satisfied. She is light skinned with long hair that is the obvious result of "race mixing." All the Black men lust after her and the white men say things like, "She looks good for a nigger woman." When raped by the white men it is not considered as such because it is said she wants sex and flaunts herself. Though the only characterized image of Black female beauty, Jezebel represents the desire of Black women by white men in general.

Little Nigger Boy/Pickaninny: a small, silly, fun-loving child who constantly gets into mischievous trouble. His/her hair is matted or in rough pigtails. S/he wears bright, clownish clothes and is dim-witted, like a family pet.

Buck: a very big, muscular, strong field slave who can be violent to other slaves and sometimes needs to be whipped to be kept in line. He is the type of slave who brought about an industry of tough white men called "Nigger Breakers." He is the type of slave owners brag about and breed saying they have the biggest, strongest slave around who can out-bale anybody. He is dumb and strong and sometimes surly. He is the only young, Black male figure, as well as the only sexualized male, but is cast as an "animal." He is a subhuman, a horse to run, work, and breed. He is no real threat to the slave owner because he is dumb, likes to work and make babies, and when violent, it is only against his own people. He has a deep fear of whites.

Coon: Blacks were called Coons after raccoons because: 1) in darkness only the raccoon's eyes are seen because they are surrounded by white fur (e.g., the stereotype about dark-skinned Black people being "so dark . . ."), and 2) like raccoons, Blacks are seen as being sneaky and stealthy (e.g., the Ku Klux Klan and white bigots referred to lynchings and hunts for Black "fugitives" as "coon huntin").

Spade derives from the black color of spades in a deck of cards. In most states the law stated if a person was 1/16th Black (one of your great-great-grandparents was Black), s/he was Black. In other states and countries the percentage was 1/8th (one of great-grandparents), one drop of blood, or some other legal racial classification. The shorthand, universal designation was simply: "Call a spade a spade."

Jigaboo: said to come from the image of Blacks "dancing a jig."

Spearchucker: until very recently, one of the worst insults in the Black community was to call someone "African" or "African Booty-Scratcher," or to tell someone "You got a bone in your nose." Spearchucker is part of this phenomenon, as is Jungle-Bunny. It connects Blacks to an African history that has been steeped in savagery, cannibalism, evil, ignorance, and darkness—one that both Blacks and whites have been brainwashed to believe is true.

Alabama Porch Monkey: a fake scientific term coming from the idea that Blacks are monkeys. But because they are not in Africa they cannot be African Jungle Monkeys, so are instead monkeys, from Alabama, found on porches. In many cartoons, Black people are portrayed as monkeys.

Stepin Fechit (as in Step and Fetch It): a Hollywood character who personified Jim Crow and others. He was depicted as a gopher. Stepin Fechit was asked as he walked barefoot with his shoes slung over his shoulder, "Hey, how come you don't wear your shoes?" He replied, "'Cause I'm savin' 'em for when my feets wears out."

• • •

These Blackface characters quickly moved from the Vaudeville stages of the early 20th century to Hollywood screens. Disney produced many cartoons filled with minstrel characters. The song "Zip-a-dee-Doo-Dah, Zip-a-Dee-Day" about how great Dixie (the South) was and how wonderful were the days of slavery, was sung by an Uncle Tom–like figure. In the original film version, the figure walks through the plantation followed by a crowd of Pickaninnies. These images are also seen in cartoons, such as *Tom & Jerry*, until the 1980s. In 1914, D. W. Griffith created *The Birth of a Nation*, a film showing what would happen if Reconstruction had continued and Blacks had gained true power:

> In the film, Black people took control of the government and made new laws. They didn't wear shoes in the House of Representatives and Senate, and ate fried chicken and watermelon for every meal. They slept, let the government fall apart, and attacked white women. In the end, the saviors (the Ku Klux Klan) came to restore honor and integrity to the country and to white women specifically. (The separation of Blacks and whites was fundamentally about the fear of Black men by white

men. Among other things, Black men were perceived as sexually desiring white women.) There is an image in the film of a "Black" man touching, chasing, and raping a white woman. While all the other Black characters are played by Blacks, this character is a white man in Blackface because Black men were not allowed to touch a white woman. President Teddy Roosevelt said the film was a breakthrough and that "all American school children" should see the film. The NAACP organized national protests.

There is a long history of Black people shucking, jiving, and making white folks smile to get ahead. During slavery, and then segregation, Blacks acted simple and jovial in order to survive. In most parts of the South until the 1940s, Blacks were expected to step off the street to allow whites to pass. Their demeanor was supposed to be, hat in hand, grinning, "Yah Suh, Na Suh, Anythin' ya need Sah." This behavior was a mask that allowed Black people to live in a racist society. **Hattie McDaniel** was the most famous and wealthiest Black actor of her time. In her Academy Award winning performance in *Gone With the Wind*, she was the personification of Aunt Jemima—a loyal, sassy maid. When she was condemned by others for playing such stereotypical characters she responded, "I'd rather make $7,000 a week playing a maid, than be a maid making $7 a week."

Demeaning images of Black characters continued in movies, television shows, and cartoons without change until the 1970s. Then subtle changes were made, slight retooling, but the images remained very much the same: the rapist, the wild nigger, the buffoon, the motherly asexual loyal and sassy woman, the jezebel, and the old loyal Black man. As Chuck D. of Public Enemy said: "You gotta learn. They still rockin' Aunt Jemima, but now she got a perm." In the history of the Academy Awards no Black person has ever won for Best Director. In the 80-year-history of the awards fewer than 10 have won for acting: Hattie McDaniel, **Sidney Poitier** (Best Supporting Actor, *Lilies of the Field*), **Denzel Washington** (Best Supporting Actor, *Glory*; Best Actor, *Training Day*), **Louis Gossett Jr.** (Best Supporting Actor, *An Officer and a Gentleman*), **Whoopi Goldberg** (Best Supporting Actress, *Ghost*), **Cuba Gooding Jr.** (Best Supporting Actor, *Jerry Maguire*), **Haile Berry** (Best Actress, *Monster's Ball*), **Jamie Foxx** (Best Actor, *Ray*), **Jennifer Hudson** (Best Actress, *Dreamgirls*), and **Forest Whitaker** (Best Actor, *The Last King of Scotland*). Most of the acting awards were given out from the mid-1990s on.

·····
RESOURCES

For Featured Workshops

Bamboozled
A film by Spike Lee
40 Acres & a Mule Productions

The Fire Next Time
"Letter to My Nephew on the One
Hundredth Anniversary of the Emancipation"
James Baldwin

Oríkí

The Importance of Oríkí in Yoruba Mural Art in
Ijele: Art eJournal of the African World
Stephen Folárànmí
www.africaresource.com

See also: http://humanityquest.com/themes/
inspiration/Languages/Yoruba/index.asp

Real Women Have Curves
A film by Patricia Cardoso
HBO Independent Productions and
LaVoo Productions

General

Anthologies

*Women Writing Resistance: Essays on Latin
America and the Caribbean*
Jennifer Browdy de Hernandez

Sacred Bond: Black Men and Their Mothers
Keith Brown

*Latino Boom: An Anthology of
U.S. Latino Literature*
John Christie, Jose Gonzalez (Eds.)

*The Eyes on The Prize Civil Rights Reader:
Documents, Speeches and Firsthand Accounts
from the Black Freedom Struggle, 1954–1990*
Clayborne Carson, David J. Garrow, Gerald
Gill, Vincent Harding, Darlene Clark Hine
(General Eds.)

*This Bridge Called My Back,
Writings by Radical Women of Color*
Cherríe Moraga

*Colonize This! Young Women of Color
on Today's Feminism*
Daisy Hernández, Bushra Rehman (Eds.)

Revolution: Faces of Change
John Miller, Aaron Kennedi (Eds.)

*Mamá: Latina Daughters Celebrate
Their Mothers*
Maria Perez-Brown

Cultural Events

High 5 Tickets to the Arts is a nonprofit organization dedicated to making the arts affordable for teens. Through High 5, teens ages 13 to 18 can buy $5 tickets to the best of New York City dance, music, theater, and visual arts events all year round
www.highfivetix.org

Education & Teaching

A Puerto Rican in New York and Other Sketches
Jesus Colon
(See also http://pages.prodigy.net/gramsci7/_import/pages.prodigy.net/gramsci7/index2.html)

Pedagogy of the Oppressed
Paolo Friere

Why We Teach
Sonia Nieto

Teach Freedom: Education for Liberation in the African American Tradition
Charles M. Payne, Carol Sills Strickland (Eds.)

Young, Gifted and Black: Promoting High Achievement among African-American Children
Theresa Perry, Claude Steele,
Asa Hilliard III (Eds.)

Pan African & Latino/a History and Culture

Africana: The Encyclopedia of the African and African American Experience
Kwame Anthony Appiah, Henry Louis Gates (Eds.)

BlackLiterature.com

Franklin H. Williams Caribbean Cultural Center/African Diaspora Institute
www.cccadi.org

Centro de Estudios de Puertoriqueños
http://centropr.org/home.html

LasCulturas.com

The Schomburg Center for Research in Black Culture
www.nypl.org/research/sc/sc.html

Slavery in America
www.slaveryinamerica.org

3

Let My Soul Spit*: **Nurturing Reflection**

> *I type in one place, but I write all over the house.*
> **Toni Morrison**

Reflection is an intentional process. It requires we build in time and create an environment conducive for thinking about what we are learning, seeing, or experiencing. Building on the learning environment created by **Setting the Tone** and on the recommended information and forms of inquiry outlined in **Content, Perspective, Dialogue**, this chapter focuses on activities that will get young people in the right frame of mind for doing reflective writing. It offers techniques that foster listening to one's inner voice and the perspectives of others.

Some young people naturally enjoy writing, and others do not. Their degree of interest is likely shaped by how well they think they can write, whether they feel they have something meaningful to express, and how much they are engaged by particular writing assignments. Messages they receive in school about their writing coming in the form of grades and praise or negative critique no doubt carry a great deal of weight. The Brotherhood/Sister Sol views reflective writing as an activity of critical exploration. The journey, as opposed to a literary outcome or positive assessment, is important unto itself as a means for processing information and perceptions. Each reflective writing activity may not lead to a strong essay or poem, but it will support critical thinking. With enough practice and guidance, young people will develop creative, well-written, and compelling work.

> Reflective writing helps young people tap into their feelings, articulate a point of view, and practice creative expression.

* To *"spit"* is to read or recite a poem or spoken word piece.

Regardless of the workshop topic or activity, there is almost always opportunity to weave in reflective writing, though to keep activities fresh, it should probably not be incorporated into every workshop. Reflective writing assignments can be designed to help young people tap into their feelings, articulate a point of view, or practice creative expression. The idea is to help them make the content their own through finding personal connections to it and through being critical of and inspired by what they are learning. The fact that their ideas and creativity are being valued, invariably increases their interest in writing. Their writing also offers insight into the real lives of young people, helping facilitators become more sensitive to their interests, fears, strengths, and struggles.

ILLUSTRATION: *It was a sunny though chilly day, and sisters of all ages were bundled up in sweatpants, hoodies, and bandannas sporting the retreat's theme:* Define Ourselves for Ourselves. *Some of our members were especially looking forward to the writing activity. For those attending their first retreat, it would be another new experience the weekend offered them. After receiving a writing packet and being given instructions, each sister found a spot she could call her own. A few stayed near to where the group would meet up in half an hour. Others sought solitude farther away, to sit atop a large boulder under an overhanging branch, or beside a rolling creek, or in the middle of a vast green meadow, each alone with her thoughts and feelings. When the group came back together several sisters volunteered to share their words. The voices that streamed forth from being quiet and solitary were honest, insightful, poignant. Young women, even those with the hardest edge, freely expressed a pain that had been wearing on them, or self-pride and awe in having climbed to a peak where they could see the full lay of the land. And they offered appreciation for sisters who stood by them through the weekend's challenges and through so many others before.* (See Retreat Reflections on the next page.)

• • • • •

WILDERNESS RETREAT REFLECTIONS
The following reflections were given in anonymously.

Sisterhood isn't just a word, it is a state of mind. It is a true blessing. It is a crown that is earned and must be worn proud. You have to rock it right. Every single one of my sisters here are doing more than giving it justice. And not only are our chapter leaders teaching us the numerous, countless ways to be a sister but they are teaching us how to spread and share sisterhood. I only hope that I am learning how to rock it and that I will be able to share it. I am truly and deeply in love with Sister Sol. Ashé. **Sister Sol**

I learned a lot from this retreat. I learned what you do is up to you. Life is up to you. What path you take, what road you walk. This is the most important thing I will take home. All of my personal demons I will put behind me from now on. I will not let fear, guilt, laziness, or anything else hold me. I will do what I need to do for me, my family, and all my brothers and sisters that are not blood. I will be mentally strong, physically strong, and spiritually strong. I will be a man. **Brotherhood**

Every time I come to a retreat, what really gets me is the Talking Circle around the campfire. I can never really leave if it's not with tears in my eyes. Sometimes when I look at a person I don't really see what's inside. You look at them from the outside and they seem to have it all together when in fact it's not the case. What I was really thinking throughout the campfire listening to the girls speak was admiration. They are young, but for young women they are very wise and I know if they keep at the pace they are going, they are going to be okay. As for me, I know I'm going to be alright too. **Sister Sol**

This is one of the greatest moments of my life. The bonfire was one of the most spiritual moments of my life. Even though I didn't say much I learned a lot from my brothers in Intrinsic Kings and Eternally Unbreakable, and this trip has made us closer and we all made one big step toward becoming men. When I go home my mind will be totally different from when I left. I am really going to start going after my priorities. **Brotherhood**

In addition to providing physical space and time for reflection, it is important to provide young people with direction for their writing and opportunities for them to receive constructive feedback. Nurturing reflection is a group activity as much as an individual act. Getting constructive feedback and hearing viewpoints from peers and facilitators having diverse backgrounds, interests, and preferences provides young writers with multiple ways for assessing their voice. They learn that the value of public critique is not from learning what is "good/right" or "bad/wrong" about their writing, but in recognizing how different people are affected by their words and that varied perspectives inform their thinking.

> The value of public critique is not from learning what is "good/right" or "bad/wrong" about one's writing, but in seeing how different people are affected by one's words.

Expression

Feeling safe to **EXPRESS** oneself gives rise to publicly testing ideas and opinions through spoken and written dialogue. Public expression fosters **EMPATHY**. **EMPATHY** fosters confidence in free **EXPRESSION**.

Empathy

ILLUSTRATION: *Lyrical Circle (our alumni poetry collective) met every Friday over five years to develop their writing. LC, as it is affectionately called, was more than a writing group. With so much time together, their bonds ran deep. Members and staff attended important events in each other's lives: birthday celebrations, funerals, graduations. An LC member writes that the space "allows one to share openly, creating a feeling of freedom. The weight of the world [is suddenly] off one's back." Another member describes the role of each LC facilitator, saying, "I was writing for about 7 years prior to LC's creation, but my focus was on myself (and whatever pain I was dealing with at the time). Working with Jacques, I learned how to improvise writing a piece. He was always random in selecting assignments, which manifested in my ability to write a thematic piece at the drop of a dime. Now with Silvia, she always allowed the space for the most conversation at LC, the topic at the time would become the next assignment, and the convo was always deep, even if it was a lighthearted discussion. Her nurturing demeanor and desire to help us with whatever we needed and to hook us up with opportunities to spit has been surpassed by none. DaMond brought out the performer in a few of us. He definitely brought me to a place where I could channel my innermost pain, and translate it to the stage. Working with Bro/Sis has turned our potential talent into control over our artistic futures."*

THE MEANING OF WRITERS' COLLECTIVE

Marsha Jean-Charles, Liberation Program, International Study Program (Brasil 2006, Ghana 2007), Writers' Collective

This group means an opportunity to
let angst, anger, hope, dismay
& all else come out.
It is a means of surviving
in a time when I feel no one else is listening.
It is a cadre of young people
who subject the ears, hearts and minds
of others to listening to their
poetic bliss for only
a few moments.
Our minds are open to new ideas,
hot lines, fresh phrases.
Our hearts are opened to witnessing
the experience of others &
the occasional realization that
others are going through the same thing.
The group provides the aura in which
I feel free to express.
Express my mind, my soul, my world.
This group shares stories of the country/city/world
in the fast lane moving too quickly to see its downfall . . .
This group is my release
where I feel free to pull the trigger
& let my soul spit.

82

• • • • •

STRATEGIES for
Nurturing Reflection

1. Set the mood.

Every person likes to write (read or study) in his or her own way. Some of us prefer sitting at a desk, others like sitting in a cozy chair. Working in schools and community organizations there are limitations to the type of spaces and furnishings we can offer young people. We can, however, allow them to find a space where they feel most comfortable and create a mood most conducive to reflecting.

Have young people find their "spot." Young people should be able to choose a space that offers them some privacy, does not allow them to see each other's work, minimizes distractions, is physically comfortable, and keeps them focused on the task. In our brownstone and in the classrooms we use in our partner schools, our members can sit anywhere they want as long as they are as far apart from each other as is possible. They might sit at a desk, on the floor, or curled up in a chair. During park outings or on wilderness retreats we instruct our members to find a solitary spot that they like and where they will not be too far from the group.

83

Consider sound or silence. During reflective writing activities there are times when we ask for complete silence, or when music is playing in the background (be it something we know young people enjoy or a genre we want to expose them to). Both silence and music create a mood. Depending on the difficulty of the activity and the particular group's ability to focus, one or the other may be preferable. Somewhat related is that young people will finish the writing assignment at different times and may need to be reminded to keep the noise down so that others can continue working on their pieces. The point here is to pay attention to the role and impact of sound.

2. Provide sufficient time and opportunity for young people to express and process their ideas and feelings.

A two-hour workshop for our members in the 7th and 8th grades can seem very long to them. They are at an age when they have tremendous amounts of physical energy and raging hormones, and are easily distracted. Our 9th- and 10th-grade members are generally able to focus on content for longer periods and have become more intentionally reflective. They are developing an interest in examining issues in detail and are more practiced at articulating their ideas and feelings. Two-hour-long workshops go by quite quickly. By the 11th and 12th grades our members are rarely aware of the time; consequently workshops are easily three hours long. Below are some strategies for providing structure and time for reflection.

Critical thinking cannot be rushed. Whatever the developmental stage of the group, the opportunity to reflect and exchange ideas should not be rushed. Do not abruptly end a dynamic discussion just because the allotted time for the workshop has passed. When reading together, include time for reviewing difficult words and concepts. During *lecturettes* (short presentations that provide information, facts, stats, etc.) encourage youth to ask questions and offer comments. Getting through the content is less important than having them understand what it is they are learning. If we recognize that our members are grasping the material but have many comments about it, we may ask them to jot down their thoughts and hold them for later discussion. If the workshop must end on time, we usually return to the topic during the next meeting. The topic might be used as a focus for *Check-in* or explored prior to the planned activity.

Get everyone involved. Critical thinking develops from questioning and testing ideas. The most interesting and enlightening workshops are interactive. Young people's participation is vital for their own development and improves facilitators' practice as they make on-the-spot modifications to ensure information is being conveyed clearly, accurately, and creatively. Try using a repertoire of strategies from having youth voluntarily speak up, to calling on them, to having everyone participate by going around the circle until everyone has contributed. Having young people raise their hands keeps the most avid speakers from monopolizing the discussion, while calling on individual members forces less outgoing youth to participate. It may be necessary to ask a young person to summarize her opinion to allow time for others to contribute to the dialogue. Having youth discuss the workshop topic in pairs prior to a large group discussion ensures each person has a chance to get involved. The strategies for inquiry described in **Content, Perspective, Dialogue** offer prompts to push and help clarify young people's thinking. And as previously mentioned, a young person should never be intentionally embarrassed, annoyed, or angered by being called on. Facilitators should, however, challenge everyone to offer their unique insight and work on their communication and critical thinking skills.

At times silence *is* golden. We do not perceive moments of silence as unproductive since it provides time for young people to think and supports the practice of "step up, step back" (described in **Setting the Tone**). After posing a question, allow time for your group to process their ideas and to hear from youth usually less quick to contribute. The silence may be uncomfortable, but it inspires thoughtful conversation and the participation of more reserved youth.

ILLUSTRATION: *A Sister Sol member had a habit of responding to every question she was asked with "I don't know." It never failed that after a few seconds of grappling with her words she would offer some profound insight. This was a pattern she repeated over and over during program activities and in casual conversation. A Chapter Leader put a challenge to her. She began by telling the young sister that she noticed how she initially responded to a question, and then went on to say she appreciated the perspectives the young woman offered despite first saying she "didn't know." The Chapter Leader then asked her to practice being silent for a moment after being asked a question, to refrain from saying, "I don't know" before responding. The young sister soon became aware of her visceral response and is steadily meeting the challenge by giving herself time to clarify her thoughts.*

Bro/Sis teens collaborating on a project.

3. Facilitate group writing.

Writing in a setting in which young people have developed strong bonds, mutual respect, and shared expectations creates an environment of positive peer pressure. By being surrounded by peers engaged in the same activity and having similar intent, young people inspire each other to stay on task and create good work. One of our members writes:

ILLUSTRATION: *I wrote because the people in the circle were really good and I wanted to be as good. I wrote because I was expected to have at least one assignment weekly, and it was enjoyable homework. I wrote because the discussions made me want to put everything I felt, and thought, and saw into words. I wrote because people listened, people told me I was good, and because I was told it mattered. I would have been a writer despite The Brotherhood/Sister Sol, but they taught me discipline and they set up an environment that made me grow.*

Mix individual reflection with group exchanges. During our wilderness retreats, each member is given a packet with an evaluation form and questions asking them to reflect on the experience (see Reflections on page 79). A similar writing activity can be facilitated, for example, during an outing to explore the neighborhood surrounding your school or organization, to a gallery or museum exhibit, or to a zoo or botanical garden. Distribute pads and pens to your group and toward the end of the outing instruct them to find their "spot." Depending on how much time you have, give them 10–20 minutes to reflect on the experience before returning to a designated location. You can keep the assignment open-ended (young people can write whatever comes to mind related to the outing) or offer guiding questions: *What is something new that you learned or experienced? What was the value of the outing? What was it like to use [the neighborhood, gallery, zoo] as a learning environment?* When your group has reassembled, ask for volunteers to share their writing, providing time for comments, questions, and dialogue.

EXCERPTS FROM THE INTERNATIONAL STUDY PROGRAM GROUP JOURNAL

Africa . . . Africa . . . Africa
Africa . . . Mother . . . Africa
take me in your warm embrace
back to my rightful place
Light this fire within my soul
This fire I thought the world could not hold
Light my path where I am to walk
Like the path where my ancestors walk
Light me like the moon in the sky . . .
Andrew Ensley, Ghana 2007

I hope this trip has changed me in many ways and that I come back home and tell a story about what I learned from this trip because this is a once in a lifetime thing. . . . When they say there is no return [referring to The Door of No Return at Cape Coast Slave Castle], well we're here baby. We're back and we're stronger. **Chantell Johnson,** Ghana 2007

Being in South Africa has inspired me to think globally when it comes to helping people, not only to think about Washington Heights but to grasp the enormous need for NGOs all over the globe. Having to interact with street children has transformed my values and beliefs. Helping people is not just handing them money but investing time in progressive change that can really transform the status quo of poverty. **Frank Lopez,** South Africa 2005

This one woman Maria and myself got engaged in a very intense and much needed conversation that other people need to have about violence in Brazil, and how she feels about life here. Just talking to her added to my evidence that I have received throughout this trip. She taught me a lot and I enjoyed it. **Dominique Mitchell,** Brasil 2006

I could write pages on the info [we learned] but it all gave me more awareness and appreciation of where I came from, and I realize that you can never know enough about yourself—there's always more to discover.
Yokasta Tineo, Dominican Republic/Puerto Rico 2003

4. Use diverse methods to unlock young people's ideas.

Freewriting: When young people are not immediately inspired by a writing assignment, freewriting can get their ideas flowing. After giving them a topic or question, instruct them that once they start writing they should continually write even if it means repeating the same thought over and over again. More often than not, they will have soon written a paragraph, then another. It may not result in the most profound or well-crafted piece, but they will have reflected on the workshop or activity. (See also *Word Riff* on page 65.)

Group journaling: Have your group collaborate on writing by taking daily or weekly turns contributing to a journal. The focus can be on collecting young people's evolving knowledge and opinions about the topic of a workshop series or about a semester-long theme or project. On completing the journal activity, make

> Group journaling records emerging knowledge and perspectives. It can also enlighten facilitators to issues affecting individual members and the group as a whole.

a copy of it for each group member as we do for members and staff participating in our **International Study Program** (see the previous page for Group Journal excerpts). More than recording what happened each day, the entries are observations about what is being experienced: *What did the day's experience mean to them? How did it make them feel? What have they learned?* The ISP journal becomes a very personal souvenir members and staff enjoy reading weeks and years after the program has ended.

Visual Aids: Creating and discussing art is a great tool for stimulating young people's thinking. When a Sister Sol chapter was having difficulty coming up with their definitions for sister, woman, and leader, their Chapter Leaders had them create collages depicting their beliefs about each concept. What they could not put into words, they were able to describe visually. Use drawing, collage making (magazine clippings, colored paper), and digital photography to elicit young people's creative and critical thinking. Because many youth will not feel comfortable about their artistic skills, focus on their ideas. How well they draw is not important. Finished work can be displayed, and each person given time to describe it to the group. (See the workshop **Art Herstory** that follows in Workshops for an example of an art-related activity.)

Role-play: Most young people enjoy developing and acting out a character or concept. We frequently have our members do role-playing or create public service announcements (PSAs) as a way to synthesize their understanding about and develop a response to a workshop topic. A PSA activity can focus on almost any topic. Young people could advocate for free speech or a presidential candidate, or they could promote a nutritious lifestyle or the concept of unity. During a workshop on sexual assault and violence that included statistical data, our members created a 1-minute PSA for their peers using what they considered to be the most important information. Our Liberation Program Collective did a group reading of Octavia Butler's novel *Kindred*. To reflect on the book's themes, they improvised a skit in the middle of the Bro/Sis office. Their skit was a form of *invisible theatre* in which the "audience" is unaware that a performance is taking place. (Invisible theatre has been used as an organizing tool for engaging the public on political and social issues.) After the performance, actors stepped out of character to facilitate a discussion on what happened and to cull the "audience's" response to it. During role-playing activities it is important for facilitators to pay attention to young people's portrayals. *How correct is the information they are conveying? How truthful or accurate, judgmental or stereotypical are their characterizations?* Following the activity, include time for the group to give each other feedback. *What are two things that worked well? What are two things that could be improved?*

WORKSHOPS

Overview: The workshops in this chapter offer approaches for helping youth connect the "self" to the "collective." The first is a short exercise for reflecting on the meaning of physical space, personally and for the larger community (see "La Casa Workshop" below). The second utilizes historical information to explore themes common to the work of women artists of color. It highlights a museum exhibition of the Black visual artist Kara Walker. Concepts of identity and privilege are examined in the third workshop through learning key terms and by doing role-playing and writing. The workshops are:

- o My Space/Our Space
- o Art Herstory 101: The Power of the Personal Narrative
- o Identity, Power, Oppression

LA CASA WORKSHOP   91

This building means a lot. The building is the first piece in the realization of a dream. A dream that our organization will spread like a plague, infecting all people, of all ethnic backgrounds and social status, both young and old, with compassion. We will help bring about lives without the views of sexism, racism, and prejudice that run rampant in our land. We will help to make the phrase "peace on earth" a reality. I hope this will be realized in my lifetime.

As for the immediate future, I hope the building will be a positive beacon in a once and proud neighborhood and begin the renaissance anew. What will I contribute to this building? To that question I can only say that too long have we sat idly by and let our negative control the positive. With this first piece created we shall reach our goal. Because we are diplomats and scholars, artists and warriors, leaders and revolutionaries, we are Brotherhood, we are Sister Sol. **Jared Brown,** Invincible/Untouchable Chapter

My Space/Our Space
(about 45 minutes to 1 hour)
Materials: writing paper, pens

Objective: This workshop grew out of our move to our then new brownstone headquarters. The Brotherhood/Sister Sol had previously been housed in a university that was not designed to accommodate teenagers and their needs. In preparing for our move we asked out members to reflect on what it would mean to have a space we could call our own (see *La Casa* on previous page). We have adapted the *La Casa* workshop here to help young people reflect on their school or community and consider what makes these seminal spaces special to or problematic for them. The purpose of this activity is to help youth pay closer attention to and define their role within their surroundings.

1. Introduction (10 minutes)—Engage your group in a brief discussion about personal and public spaces (school, home, library, playground, youth center, bedroom). Ask them to identify the various settings they encounter each day and to think about those in which they feel most and least comfortable.

2. Reflective Writing (15–20 minutes)—Distribute pens and paper and have your group write about a private or public space of their choosing by considering the following:

> What does it look like and how is it used?
> What would it mean if it no longer existed?
> Does it make you feel safe or not?
> Do you have input in how it looks or feels?
> How do you, or could you, contribute to the space?

3. Reading Exchange (20–25 minutes)—Have each person pass his or her writing to the person to their left to read aloud, reminding them to be respectful about reading each other's work. (Refer to your *Rules of Conduct*.) Allow time for the group to ask questions or clarify details.

Rap-up (15 minutes)—Have a general discussion about the assignment and reflections.

Art Herstory 101: The Power of the Personal Narrative

(3 hours or five 45-minute sessions)

Materials: information about Frida Kahlo and Kara Walker and selections of their art, information about Margaret Garner and Saartjie Baartman, excerpts from *Roots* by Alex Haley, markers, white and colored paper, scissors (Also see Resources.)

Objective: This workshop was created to coincide with the exhibit ***Kara Walker: My Complement, My Enemy, My Oppressor, My Love*** (Whitney Museum of American Art, New York City, 2007–2008). Walker was the first young black female artist given a full-scale exhibition at a major New York museum. Her work is situated in the era of American slavery and the period immediately following the Emancipation Proclamation. Because of its controversial imagery (e.g., silhouettes of cut-outs representing different "characters" from the antebellum period engaged in violent and misogynistic and sexual acts), it is necessary to contextualize Walker's work to help young people process its social and historical messages. Including the Mexican artist Frida Kahlo offers another example of a woman artist of color who expressed deep feelings rooted in culture and history, love and pain. Referencing Saartjie Baartman (the so-called Hottentot Venus) and Margaret Garner (the model for Sethe in Toni Morrison's novel *Beloved*) illustrates the dehumanizing effect of slavery and objectification and exploitation of Black women from the 18th century to today. Lastly, this workshop additionally helps young people explore artistic self-expression.

Preparation: View and select work (about 5–10 pieces) from the Kara Walker exhibit (online or in the printed exhibition catalog) and Frida Kahlo, and compile information about their lives into a one- to two-page biography to distribute to your group. You might also compile excerpts from the *Diary of Frida Kahlo*. Research the stories of Margaret Garner and Saartjie Baartman and compile the information into handouts as well.

Workshop

1. Frida (30 minutes)—Distribute and have volunteers take turns reading the biographic information you compiled on Frida Kahlo, then have your group identify what stood out to them about her life. Next, display Kahlo's art you selected without showing your group their titles and give them time to look at each work closely. Have your group share their thoughts about the meaning of the pieces. Help them make connections between Kahlo's life story and her paintings (e.g., her very vivid and candid self-expressions). Review excerpts from her diary to bring out how her daily thoughts were consumed with her husband the artist Diego Rivera, as well as her chronic physical pain. You can also read Kahlo's statement below and have your group discuss its meaning:

"I paint self-portraits because I am the person I know best. I paint my own reality."

2. Margaret Garner (20 minutes)—Distribute the information you compiled on Margaret Garner and have your group take turns reading it aloud. Help them reflect on the level of desperation and sacrifice that would drive a mother to kill her child as Garner did. Discuss how slavery was a dehumanizing institution that led to dysfunctional relationships between and among enslaved people and their enslavers. You can also use excerpts from *Roots* (pgs 454–455, 464–465) to further illustrate the horrors of slavery.

3. Tie-In (15 minutes)—Distribute the information you compiled on Kara Walker for your group to take turns reading aloud. Highlight some of the themes she addresses in her work and help your group make connections to the ideas you discussed about Frida Kahlo and Margaret Garner. Here, you can also use information you gathered about Saartjie Baartman to further bring out the historical objectification and exploitation of Black women.

4. Kara Walker (30–45 minutes)—Sister Sol members had the benefit of being able to tour Kara Walker's exhibition. For your group, display the images you selected of Walker's work and give them time to examine them closely. Have them jot down their observations and questions as they "tour" the display. Next, facilitate a discussion about Walker that, as with Kahlo, allows your group to identify what stood out to them about her life and share their thoughts about the meaning of the pieces. Help them to also make connections between Kahlo's life story and her paintings.

5. Reflective Art Activity (30 minutes)—Ask members to draw their own self-portraits. Remind them that a self-portrait does not have to be a literal depiction of what they look like, but like Frida's work, can reflect the way they feel about themselves and their lives at the current moment. Once everyone is finished, display the pieces and give your group time to examine them, then have each person share and discuss her self-portraits. Time permitting, you can ask each person to write a short narrative about her self-portrait and/ or to reflect on the workshop. Consider following up this workshop with a viewing of and discussion about the feature film *Frida*.

Identity, Power, Oppression

(Two 2-hour workshops or about six 45-minute sessions)

Materials: marbles, small bowl, writing paper, large paper, markers, pens, *Post-It* notes, copies of workshop HANDOUTS on pages 98–100 (Also see Resources.)

Objective: This workshop will help young people: 1) explore how our identities are shaped and related to our position in society, community, and the world; 2) identify and understand the different communities to which we belong; 3) identify how different forms of oppression impact our communities and lives.

Workshop

1. Who Are You? (35–45 minutes)—Explain to your group that the workshop focuses on the intersection between identity, power, and oppression by first exploring their individual identities. Give them a few minutes to think about an important article of clothing, jewelry, or another item and to think about: *Why is it important? What would happen if they didn't have it any more? Would they be different without it?* Next, distribute the Identity Worksheet HANDOUT and pens. Ask them to find a space where they can privately fill out the sheet. Give them about 15 minutes. Once everyone has completed his or her sheet, have them discuss these questions:

> How easy or hard is it to recognize different characteristics in a person just by looking at them?
>
> Why might it be important to talk about differences between the identity characteristics you can see and those that you cannot?
>
> How much do the characteristics the group identified define us, if at all?

2. Understanding Power (35–45 minutes)—Distribute several *Post-It* notes to each person and ask them to brainstorm words and images that come to mind when they hear the word "power." Have them write their ideas on separate *Post-It* notes, then hang them on the board to discuss together. Next, on large paper write <u>Our Power</u> on one side and <u>Their Power</u> on the other. Take a few minutes to create a list of their examples under each category. Your group may categorize <u>Our Power</u> as including their community, youth, people of color, or women, and <u>Their Power</u> as men, whites, the rich, the government. After creating the list, ask them to share any personal and observed experiences of oppression, control, or privilege. Next, have them sort their *Post-It* notes under the categories of <u>Our</u>

<u>Power</u> and <u>Their Power</u> and explain and discuss their choices. Continue the conversation to highlight how power is exercised through wealth, critical mass, and other resources and institutions in society.

3. Marbles (10 minutes)—For this activity it is important to remind your group about respecting each other's feelings and ideas and maintaining confidentiality. Let them also know that this is a silent activity. Have your group sit in a circle and distribute 15 marbles to each person. Explain that a facilitator will read statements to them (see below) and after hearing each they should throw a marble in the bowl placed in the middle of the circle if it pertains to them. When all the statements have been read, ask your group to silently observe how many marbles they and their peers still have in their hands.

> You have been embarrassed because your family did not have enough money to
> buy you most popular things.
> You or somebody in your family emigrated here from another country.
> Your parents did not go to college.
> You know someone who is an undocumented and earns less than minimum wage.
> You know someone who can't get a job because of a criminal record.
> You or someone you know is physically disabled.
> You or somebody you know sells drugs because they need the money.
> You know someone who wishes they were lighter skinned.
> You are under 18 years of age.
> You have heard jokes told about members of your racial or ethnic group.
> You have ever made fun of someone because of the way they dress.
> You have been disrespected as a woman.
> You or someone you know grew up with domestic violence in their household.
> You or someone you know has experienced sexual assault.
> You or someone you know is gay, lesbian, bisexual, queer, or transgender.

4. Reflections (20 minutes)—Provide 5–10 minutes for your group to write their thoughts about the following questions before discussing them together:

> What the activity says about the experiences of the people in this room
> What the bowl full of marbles represents
> How their identities are connected to power
> What they thought of this activity

5. Unveiling Oppression (35–45 minutes)—On a large sheet of paper write the word Oppression in the center and circle it. Then ask your group what comes to mind when they hear this word. Record their responses on the paper by connecting them to the center with a line to create a web-like diagram. Circle any examples of "isms" such as racism, sexism, ageism, etc. After gathering diverse responses, ask your group to define "ism" and identify the Power Group and Target Group. For example:

Ism	Power Group	Target Group
sexism	men	women
racism	whites	people of color
heterosexism	heterosexuals	homosexuals
ageism	adults	children/youth
classism	rich	working class

Next, on large paper write Interpersonal, Institutional, and Internal. Describe to your group what each of these means as related to oppression and power. (Refer to the Key Terms HANDOUT and see Resources at the end of this chapter.) Distribute and review the Key Terms HANDOUT and discuss the various "isms" to explain the concepts.

6. Skits (40 minutes)—Divide your group into small groups of about four and assign each a scenario (HANDOUT 3). Give them 20 minutes to develop a 2-minute skit and then have each group present its work. After each group has presented, facilitate a discussion on the following:

> Any overlapping they noticed
> Any ideas they got for using "people power" to dismantle oppression
> What it was like creating a skit with their group
> What they thought of this activity

Rap Up (20–30 minutes)—Bring this workshop series to a close with a writing activity in which your group reflects on identity, power, and oppression: what they learned about it and how it personally affects them. Ask for volunteers to share their words.

Identity Worksheet

Fill out this worksheet as best you can. You will not be required to share your answers.

Sex: _____   Health: _____

Gender: _____   Appearance: _____

Sexuality: _____   Personality type: _____

Race: _____   Hair: _____

Class: _____   Language: _____

Age: _____   Blood type: _____

Skin Color: _____   Education: _____

Where you live: _____   Where you're from: _____

Body type: _____

List and complete any other categories you want to add:

_____

_____

_____

_____

Key Terms

Identity can be defined as:

1. Our unique individual traits or characteristics
2. The characteristics by which we label ourselves or are labeled by others
3. Characteristics shared by a group, community, organization, etc.

Power is the ability or official capacity to exercise control, authority; of or relating to political, social, or economic control

Institutional Power is control or authority which is exercised by a social system or institution. It is a hierarchical, or top-down, form of power.

Power of the People is control or authority in the hands of people (bottom-up), as opposed to an institution, social system, or some higher authority.

Institution is a custom, practice, relationship, or behavioral pattern of importance in a community or society; an organization, establishment, foundation, society, or the like devoted to the promotion of a particular cause or program; any established law, custom, etc.

Community is a group of people living in the same location; a group having common interests; a group viewed as forming a distinct segment of society.

Oppression is the arbitrary and cruel exercise of power resulting in classism, racism, sexism, heterosexism, ageism, etc.

The 3 'I's of Oppression

Institutional Oppression is the systematic mistreatment of people within a social identity group, supported and enforced by the society and its institutions, solely based on the person's membership in the social identity group.

Interpersonal Oppression is oppression that occurs between people who may or may not share aspects of their identity.

Internalized Oppression takes place when an oppressed individual believes and perpetuates the negative and demeaning stereotypes about her or his identity group.

SOURCES: dictionary-reference.com; The American College Dictionary;
https://edgenet.edgewood.edu/whiteprivilege/examples_of_different_forms_of_r.htm
Identity, Power, Oppression HANDOUT 2 © The Brotherhood/Sister Sol 2008

Skit Scenarios

The scenarios below are a mix of low- and high-risk situations. Those that will raise particularly sensitive feelings should be used with caution based on the ability of your group to process the topic and how deeply the group has bonded. Give them 20 minutes to develop their skit in which group members must play a role. "Performers" should not explain what their skit is about so that others can guess.

Interpersonal Sexism at School

Develop a skit that depicts a situation at a school where a young person is harassing another because of his or her gender.

— —

Internalized Racism at Home

Develop a skit that depicts a situation where a young person is admiring the physical features of someone from a privileged race, and making negative comments about her or his own race.

— —

Institutional Ageism at Work

Develop a skit that depicts a young person who needs to work in order to support his or her family, or wants to buy something from a "fancy" store, but is challenged because of his or her age.

— —

Interpersonal Heterosexism in a Locker Room

Develop a skit that depicts a situation that takes place between peers in a gym locker room or bathroom and deals with sexual differences.

— —

Internalized Classism at a Club or Party

Develop a skit that depicts a situation that takes place between two different groups waiting to be chosen to get into a party or club.

RESOURCES

For Featured Workshops

Saartjie Baartman
Hottentot Venus: A Novel
Barbara Chase-Riboud

Margaret Garner
www.aalbc.com/authors/margaret.htm
www.123exp-biographies.com/

Frida Kahlo
Diary of Frida Kahlo
Carlos Fuentes

Frida
A film by Julie Taymor

Frida: A Biography of Frida Kahlo
Hayden Herrera

Invisible Theatre
Theatre of the Oppressed
Augusto Boal and Charles McBride
See also: http://en.wikipedia.org/wiki/
Theater_of_the_Oppressed

Racism
A Race Is a Nice Thing to Have (2nd Ed.)
Janet E. Helms

See also: https://edgenet.edgewood.edu/
whiteprivilege/examples_of_different_forms_
of_r.htm)

Roots: The Saga of an American Family
Alex Haley

Kara Walker
*Kara Walker: My Complement, My Enemy, My
Oppressor, My Love*
Philippe Vergne, Sander Gilman, Thomas
McEvilley and Robert Storr

See also: www.whitney.org/www/exhibition/
kara_walker/index.html
www.pbs.org/art21/artists/walker/index.html

General

The Creative Spirit
Daniel Goleman, Paul Kaufman
and Michael Ray

*Healing Wisdom of Africa, Finding Life Purpose
Through Nature, Ritual & Community*
Malidoma Patrice Somé

Labyrinths
A meandering self-contained path leading
to a center point and used to promote
contemplation and relaxation
http://en.wikipedia.org/wiki/Labyrinth

Talking Circles
A method for promoting democratic talking
and listening that is rooted in Native
American practices
http://en.wikipedia.org/wiki/Talking_circle

4

I Want to Always Learn: **Incorporating Drafts & Revisions**

One of the most difficult things is the first paragraph.
I have spent many months on a first paragraph,
and once I get it, the rest just comes out very easily.
Gabriel García Marquez

For some of our members the thought of revising their work is not as appealing as getting their ideas down on paper. Many of the writing activities we facilitate do not have absolute deadlines. We have the luxury of time to help our members strengthen their work. Nor is every writing assignment intended to develop into a polished piece. However, if we observe interest in an assignment or see that their pieces show promise, we will have our members further develop their work. There are times when they must revise their writing until it is as perfect as can be because, for instance, it is a requirement of the assignment (such as an *Oath of Dedication*, a component of our Rites of Passage Program), it will be part of a presentation or publication, or it is an essay for their college application (assistance we offer to all our members).

By exposing young people to a range of thought-provoking literary forms (from editorials, to contemporary poetry, to great literature), facilitators are helping them see that quality writing engages readers' minds and spirits. Youth begin to appreciate that good writers choose their words very carefully and with purpose, that each has a unique focus, perspective, and rhythm (or voice). They also see that writing can be a force for social change by informing readers about important issues and ideas, connecting issues to real-life situations, and inspiring a response or action. When it is time for young people to develop their own work, they will understand that drafts and revisions are essential to creating a strong essay, poem, story, paper, or article. Receiving one-on-one support and positive, specific feedback also encourages youth to develop multiple drafts of their work. An essay or poem may require two or three drafts. A college essay may go through five or more revisions.

> Young people see that writing can be a force for social change by informing readers about important issues and inspiring them to respond or take action.

ILLUSTRATION: *During the third phase of our* Rites of Passage Program, *chapter members write an* Oath of Dedication. *In earlier phases they collaborated on creating a chapter* Mission Statement *and definitions for sister/woman/leader or brother/man/leader. The Oath is their personal testament of their life aspirations and commitments. Chapter Leaders bring their members together to explain this stage, asking them to look back before moving forward. They review steps the group has already taken with each other in building brotherhood and sisterhood bonds and becoming young men and women. They discuss the role of ritual and public presentation as a part of their transition from childhood to adulthood, and reflect on the many issues they have explored together over the years—Pan African and Latino/a history and culture, sexism, social justice—before challenging their members to put their values, dreams, and fears in writing, to dedicate themselves in word and deed to their beliefs. Over a couple of months our young sisters and brothers work on developing their Oaths, taking feedback from their peers and Chapter Leaders who know them well, shaping and honing their statement until it is a true reflection of their ideals. Their final version is printed on textured paper and framed, then presented at an* Oath of Dedication *ceremony. Many of our members hang their Oaths on their bedroom and college dorm walls.* (Read an actual Oath of Dedication on the next page.)

A Sister Sol Circle

OATH OF DEDICATION

Nakkiyya King, Eternal Sistas, After School Program, International Study Program
(Dominican Republic/Puerto Rico 2003)

I am: A young woman of color
    A home-schooled graduate
    A daughter, granddaughter, cousin, sister
    A friend

I am NAKKIYYA AMIRA KING!
I am dedicating myself to life and love. I want to be someone people can look up to. Someone who can own up to her mistakes and learns from them. I will try my hardest not to have regrets. As long as I remain true to me and do what makes me happy I will have no room for them.

I want to stay well connected with my family, especially the women. The women who have taught and continue to teach me well. The women I look up to. The women who I hope to pattern my life after. The women who I want to make proud.

I want to always be in love. Be in love with my friendships, my partner, my career, my home, my children, my family, myself.

I want to always believe. No matter what religion I practice or how hard life may get I always want to believe in a higher power. I never want to lose faith.

I want to stay open to growth and pain. I believe that with growth comes pain and with pain comes strength.

I want to always learn. I will continue my education in school. I will always read and ask questions. I will sit and listen to those who can teach me. And I will learn from my own life experiences.

I want to become my own cheerleader. I need to better motivate myself in order to further my growth. No one can support me more than me.

I want to keep giving back to my family, my true friends, my programs, and my community. It has taken all these aspects of my life to help make me who I am so far.

I am: A young woman of color
    A home-schooled graduate
    A daughter, granddaughter, cousin, sister
    A friend

I am NAKKIYYA AMIRA KING!

And so I have much more to learn . . .

$\bullet \bullet \bullet \bullet \bullet$

Strategies for
Incorporating Drafts & Revisions

1. Focus on big ideas and then the details.

One: Edit with a gentle touch. Most of us do not appreciate having our writing returned to us marked up with red ink. Read through the entire piece before noting any comments or corrections in the margins. Questions that initially arise might be addressed later in a piece. This may mean the young person needs to better organize it, but that he has a strong concept or thesis. You could also use a pencil in case you need to erase a comment you later realize is not relevant. **Two**: Identify strengths before pointing out shortcomings. Indicate *specific* sections (or even sentences) that are well written or express an interesting idea or perspective. Specificity provides clear examples and shows the young person that you have read her work carefully. **Three**: Use the questions below as a guide for offering constructive critique. **Fourth**: Give verbal feedback during one-on-one meetings.

What are you trying to say here? What do you mean by this?
What do you want the reader to understand by reading your piece?
How does your perspective or personal experience connect to others?

FIRST DRAFT

Focus on the big ideas: Identify specific well-written passages and good ideas. Clarify the focus, point of view and purpose of the piece.

SECOND DRAFT

Review edits identified in the first draft: Look for repetition. Ensure word usage accurately expresses ideas or feelings. Examine how well the ideas flow together. Make sure there is a clear beginning, middle, and ending.

THIRD DRAFT ON

Polish the piece: Review edits identified in previous drafts. Fact check. Sharpen grammar. Spell check. Make sure formatting is consistent.

2. Emphasize the power of words.

Writers choose their words with intention, to make a particular point, play with double meanings, and/or provoke ideas, feelings, or action. The revision process is an opportunity for paying close attention to the power of one's words. Though our members are not allowed to use *nigger*, *bitch*, and *faggot* at The Brotherhood/Sister Sol because they work against developing a culture of solidarity and caring, we do not censor their writing. We challenge them to find creative ways of expressing themselves by choosing words with specific intent (even the three taboo ones). Having taken time to get to know young people familiarizes facilitators with their use of language or way of speaking. This knowledge is important to take into account when offering critique. For example, in the writing sample on page 91, Jared uses the word "plague" to mean something positive, similar to how "bad" or "ill" means "good" or "cool." Questions that will help young people carefully choose their words:

What emotions are you trying to express?

What feeling or response are you trying to elicit?

Can you think of another way to say this? What words have the same meaning or offer similar impact?

(Hint: Have a dictionary and thesaurus handy.)

107

3. Form, focus and fact checking.

After learning about the strengths of their writing and where it needs additional work, the young person should have sufficient guidance to work on a second draft. (Make sure he has been taking good notes.) Depending on the length and complexity of the piece, the young person may eventually submit a series of revisions. With each review, feedback becomes more specific. Other questions that will help young people hone their writing are:

Does your piece have a clear beginning, middle, and end?

How well have you stayed focused on your topic?

Imagine your readers knows nothing about your topic. How well would your piece inform them about it?

Is your information accurate? Have you checked your facts?

How well have you presented and argued your point of view? How well do you think your piece provokes or inspires?

4. Provide opportunity for group critiques.

When young people and facilitators know each other well, group critiques offer constructive feedback sensitive to the writer's true voice. Group critiques can take place at the beginning or at a later stage of a writing assignment, but it is always important to remind your group of the basic ground rules it has already established (e.g., listening with respect, no side conversations, not attacking the person, etc.). Additionally, ask youth to start off with positive feedback before offering respectful criticism. We facilitate group critiques by having our members read their work to each other, always clapping after each young person has presented. Depending on the time frame, young people will read all or part of their piece or only a few volunteers will share. Our members also read each others' work aloud. Have your group pass their pieces to the person to their left, or alternatively, collect their writing and pass them out randomly, making sure no one gets his or her own piece back. Hearing their words being read by someone else, young people can listen to the flow or rhythm of the piece, more readily recognize mistakes, and can appreciate their work from the vantage point of being their own audience.

> Have your group start off with positive feedback. Limit constructive criticisms to about three key points as any more can be overwhelming and hard for a young person to absorb and put into practice.

108

Using art to explore ideas

5. Add the polishing touches.

Youth will need to review their work for spelling and grammatical errors and formatting. If using a computer, they will likely rely on *spell* and *grammar check*. However, writing software cannot identify synonyms or homonyms, or differentiate repetition from artistic phrasing. Encourage young people to develop the habit of having someone edit their work. Also suggest that they allow time to put their work aside for a couple of days. When they re-read it, they will be able to see their mistakes more readily.

Formatting issues address typeface, font size, indents, centering, publishing specifications, and the layout of the manuscript. Young people may need help making sure their layout is consistent and neat. Provide clear instructions for formatting, such as font style and size, or margin width. If necessary, give a tutorial on basic word processing features (e.g., centering text, using tabs, adding footnotes, etc.).

ILLUSTRATION: *The objective of a typical college essay is to have students describe what makes them unique enough to be accepted into the school to which they are applying. And this is where many young people get stumped. Many students have great difficulty identifying their special qualities for why a college would accept them at all, much less over someone else. An outcome of continual practice at writing, including group journaling, is that our members have assembled material and experience they can use for developing their college essays. A kernel of an idea, a visceral thought that lingers with them, becomes the basis for reflecting on and expressing core ideologies. Keith Brisbane's college essay on the next page is an example of a work that began as a group journal entry and merged with other ideas he was exploring. The result is a clear and strong statement in which readers hear the complex and individual thinking of this young man.*

COLLEGE ESSAY
Keith Brisbane, Intrinsic Kings Brotherhood Chapter, International Study Program (Ghana, 2007)

When I was younger all I knew of the world was what I saw along the journey between my house and my school. As I became older I learned more and more about the world through school and my own studies. But none of it was real to me. In July of 2007 I took the chance to make all those National Geographic specials real. Thanks to The Brotherhood/Sister Sol, I was able to travel to Ghana, Africa. I can say it truly was the most life-altering experience I have ever had.

I went because I yearned for and needed something different. My trip to the Motherland was a gateway to a new beginning. Everything smelled, tasted, felt, and looked new. The food was more succulent, the color of the sky was more vibrant, and everything felt right for a change. My soul, body, heart, and mind—they were all completely refreshed. I really didn't like my life in America; I was always heated and stressed because of my academic and family life. My high school has never really captured my interest or challenged me to reach my full potential. My voyage gave me time to find myself and make some serious adjustments. It helped me to reevaluate the way I treated my family, the company I kept, and my approach to school.

I was challenged mentally, physically, and spiritually during my stay in Ghana. We traveled throughout several regions of the country. My body and mind were strained because we traveled via bus and most of our destinations were usually six to eight hours apart.

We visited various landmarks, with one being the most dreadful, yet spiritually liberating places on the planet. I'm speaking of Cape Coast Castle. It is the site where millions of Africans were placed in bondage and transported through the "Middle" Passage. It is also the site where the British governor held office and where foreign students came to learn on the upper levels, while hundreds of enslaved Africans died beneath them. Everything about that place was wrong. The smell was rancid and the walls were filthy from centuries of blood and dead flesh. There were scratches on the walls where my ancestors tried to claw their way to freedom. I cried there, like I never have before. It opened me up. All of my soul poured out of me into the holding area that was the male dungeon. But my soul came back and with it a whole new outlook on life, and knowledge of who I am.

There was one village where we stayed that was named Wusuta. It is a quaint village a few kilometers inland from the main road. I was home. Wusuta is an Ewé community from which many Africans were taken, led out towards the coast to the aforementioned slave castles. Uprooted from their homes by other Africans, and then sold to marauders of the British and Portuguese variety, I felt like I was going back to the start, I was replanting those roots. I call Wusuta my African neighborhood. There was little electricity and no hot water, but I still felt good. It taught me that I really don't need all of the things I am accustomed to at home. Trivial things like computers, television, and public transportation, they all made me lazy and I had to adjust to the village lifestyle. I met people in the village that were genuinely friendly, they took care of me as if I was family, and it really felt that way.

For the final test I had to face life at home, life in America. The long and arduous plane ride gave me a lot of time to think, to think about change, about my friends and family, about my education. I've never been the studious type; my high school career was sidetracked by my frustration with the tediousness of the curriculum being taught. On the plane, on my way back, I realized that although I was intelligent I need my grades to reflect my intellect, and they do not. I was diverted away from my schoolwork because I felt that only I could develop my mind. I read a vast amount, consuming all the information held in books such as *1984* by George Orwell, James Baldwin's *Going to Meet the Man*, and Claude Brown's *Manchild in the Promised Land*. Upon my return I began reading Chinua Achebe's *Things Fall Apart*, the story of an Ibo village in present-day Nigeria. I read this novel because of my interest in the study of my people and my culture before colonialism. Reading *Things Fall Apart* and experiencing my trip back to the Motherland have given me a new direction towards the decisions I make in my life.

·····

RESOURCES

Dictionary & Thesaurus
The New Oxford American Dictionary
Merriam-Webster Spanish-English Dictionary
The Concise Roget's International Thesaurus
dictionary.reference.com
www.askoxford.com
thesaurus.reference.com
www.spanishdict.com

Grammar & Formatting
APA: The Easy Way
Peggy Houghton and Timothy J. Houghton

The Chicago Manual of Style
University of Chicago

The Elements of Style
William Strunk Jr.

5

I Do Not Have Weak Dreams: **Providing a Forum**

*As an artist I come to sing, but as a citizen, I will always speak for peace,
and no one can silence me in this.*
Paul Robeson

Youth workers and teachers looking at anthologies of our members' writings wanted to know what we were doing to get our members to write. What we saw as underlining their question was, how is The Brotherhood/Sister Sol helping young people think critically about what they are learning, reflecting on, and then writing about? The anthologies are but one of the many forums we use to continually showcase the words of our members. In many schools and families and in the public discourse, youth are talked about, but rarely heard from. Given a forum for expression, their voices ring with a clarity of personal truth and poignancy that is difficult not be moved by or to easily dismiss. We know that having their work displayed, printed, or performed enhances young people's sense of self and their respect for the ability of the written word to enlighten and inspire.

ILLUSTRATION: *During a recent* Liberating Voices/Liberating Minds Institute, *we worked with students, teachers, and the principal from a small alternative high school. They wanted a training that would help strengthen the school's sense of community that is very ethnically diverse. One student calls the school a "second chance" because it takes in students from other schools where they weren't flourishing. Students do not receive grades but earn credits for classes they need in order to graduate. As part of the training the group created a* Mission Statement *defining their shared values as a school community. When it was completed, our facilitator typed up the final version and distributed it to the group. One student looked at his copy with surprise. "We just did this?" he asked. Seeing the statement typed somehow gave the work more significance and made the young man feel proud. Later in the training, the students decided on their own to create their definitions for a student. They wrote the finished statement on large paper in colored marker and signed their names at the bottom. It now hangs in their principal's office.*

114

A collaborative performance with spoken word

STRATEGIES for
Providing a Forum

1. Collect young people's writing.

The initial step to providing a forum for young people is to make sure they hold onto their writings and keep them neat and clean. Each of our chapter members has a folder or binder in which they compile their writing and workshop handouts. The cover has the young person's name, the chapter's name, and either the *Mission Statement* or a picture of the chapter. After four to six years of Rites of Passage activities, our members have gathered an impressive collection of their writings. Even a semester or year's worth of young people's work is impressive. Give each member of your group a folder or binder she or he can decorate, and keep the folders or binders in a location the youth can easily access. Provide time for them to periodically review their collection. They will feel good that it is growing and that their writing is improving.

2. Highlight young people's words within your school or organization.

The most accessible forum for young people's writing is to feature it on the walls throughout   **115**
their schools and organizations. School assemblies and public announcements, community events and celebrations are other accessible and obvious forums. These relatively low-risk exposures deepen young people's sense of belonging and strengthen their self-confidence to take yet more intellectual and creative chances. Our members' framed *Mission Statements* and *Definitions for Sister/Woman/Leader* and *Man/Brother/Leader* surround a fireplace on the main floor of our brownstone.

LOW-RISK TO HIGH-RISK AUDIENCES
Group or Class
Organization event or School assembly
Local community
General public

3. Help young people publish and perform their work.

There are many opportunities for young people to enter poetry or spoken word contests (such as Teen Slams) and to submit their work to online or hard copy publications. These forums will broaden and diversify their exposure. See Resources on page 122 for publishing sources and contest and performance opportunities and tools.

Compile and print an anthology of young people's writing. To begin, ask young people for submissions (revised pieces of their best work). Depending on the book's anticipated length and the size of your group, three to five pieces from each person is a good range. Deciding which to include and making sure that each young person is represented will be a challenge. As a general guide, choose the best examples of each person's work, that which is well-written and expresses the young person's unique voice. Limiting the number of entries can help narrow the selection process (and reduce printing costs). After reading all the submissions, it can be helpful to identify an organizing theme or writing form (e.g., poetry, essays). (You could conceivably have chosen a theme from the start and asked young people for relevant submissions.) After making the final selections and defining a theme, dividing the writings into chapters of similar pieces will give the anthology structure and make it user-friendly. Chapter titles can be excerpts from the young people's writing (as with this curriculum).

The anthology will then need to be designed (using such software as *Word, Publisher, InDesign*, etc.) and edited (for typos, grammar, and layout). Using young people's artwork or pictures of them for the cover and/or within the book will make the book more appealing to young readers. The anthology can be photocopied, then stapled or spiral bound, or if there is funding, professionally printed. There are also online publishing options that allow you to print copies as needed. Sources for funding include foundation grants (for nonprofit organizations and schools), local businesses and grassroots fundraising (e.g., bake sales, performances, car washes, advertisements placed in the publication, etc.). Copyrighting and registering your anthology with an International Standard Book Number (ISBN) are other considerations. An ISBN is not necessary, but allows you to sell your book in retail stores.

Though facilitators offer guidance and access to resources, young people can be involved in all aspects of developing an anthology of their writing.

Encourage young people to enter contests and to take the stage.
Preparing young people for performance requires they learn how to deal with stage elements (e.g., elocution, audience, microphone, lighting, nerves). The more they know what to expect and have tools to fall back on, the stronger their performance.

Preparing for performance

Acting is action. Performers imagine, recall, and reference prior experiences that will help the words they speak resonate for themselves and their audience. A strong performance convinces, consoles, admonishes, incites. Have youth think about what inspired them to write their piece, or about a past experience or particular emotion that will bring their words to life. Ask them to envision a location, a particular time of day, or the weather or other environmental element to contextualize their memory or emotion. They can also imagine a specific audience to whom they are speaking. Perhaps the words are something they have wanted to say to a parent, friend, or adversary. Different youth will rely on different prompts, and some more than others. Using too many triggers or tapping into unresolved or raw feelings can be overwhelming. Facilitators need to pay attention to the level of emotion. Can the young person get through her piece? Is his voice cracking or is he about to cry? If you are unsure whether a young person can manage her emotions, have a private conversation to help her assess her feelings and perhaps choose another performance prompt.

A spoken word performance

Let young people know that it is okay to be nervous. Trying not to be nervous (and being told not to be) will only make a young person more so. Speaking too fast is a tactic many people use to get through their performance as quickly as possible. Unless speed is an element of the piece (as with some rapping), the quality of the performance usually suffers. Walking around the stage can also be a reaction to nerves. However, movement should be connected to dialogue or else it will look like pacing. A young person with lots of energy may need to identify specific sentences or words where it makes sense for him to move around, and then practice limiting his movements to coincide with speaking those particular words. Breathing exercises will help center young people by giving them tools for speaking clearly (e.g., elocution, pronunciation) and for calming their nerves.

Though having a podium will enable youth to quickly refer to their writing, looking down at their paper detracts from the performance. To help youth memorize their lines, have them break their piece into sections of four to five lines, practicing and memorizing each section before moving onto the next. During rehearsals, have someone "on book" (with a copy of the piece) who can give the performer a line or prompt when she gets stuck. (Connecting memory and emotion to their words will also help young people recall them.)

Working the audience

Before any performance, check out the space. Sit in the worst seat in the house and examine the view to the stage. Are there any obstructions? Have someone speak from the stage to see how sound travels. Performers may have access to a microphone. If not, they will need to project their voice so that it carries throughout the space. Advise young people to speak to the exit sign in the rear. The audience cannot be seen by the performer who is standing on a lit stage and looking into a dark theatre. "Eye contact" is instead made within the mind's eye. Rather than attempting to focus on a particular person, young people should look over or beyond the audience, keeping in mind the person/audience they imagined in their preparation.

Before going on stage, young people should take a moment to think about their piece and remind themselves of the memory or emotions tied to it. Dedicating their work to someone can keep performance of an old work fresh.

After they have been introduced, but before they begin performing, suggest that they take a deep breathe, greet the audience or briefly describe their piece (e.g., "This work comes from my experience . . ."). These techniques will help calm and center them.

Even experienced performers forget their own poem, lyrics, or lines. Remind young people that the audience will not notice mistakes unless brought to their attention. Rather than apologize, they should practice the breathing techniques they learned, resume their performance, and/or use the mistake as a dramatic pause.

OATH OF COMMITMENT
Zora Howard, Liberation Program

An *Oath of Commitment* is the culminating activity of the month-long Summer Liberation School during which LP members learn about social change movements and organizing tactics. It echoes the *Oath of Dedication* written by members in our Rites of Passage Program (see **Illustration** on page 104), but develops out of a significantly shorter process than within the Rites of Passage Program.

I don't know who got to decide my roots were too hard to comb. My father used to olive oil them every Saturday and then let me put barrettes in as I please. And I used to wear it just like that. With olive oil and bobos. The kids at school used to tell me I was too light to be black, and the ones back home used to tell me, "Stop putting all that damn suntan lotion on, your high yelluh behind could use some color." The boys on corners like when my jeans are tight, and Mommy likes it when I keep them high. Bro/Sis asked us all to write an oath stating what we commit to stand for, and I can't even decide where I stand. I think we all grow up too fast without time to look down, breathe in and realize where we have arrived. Learn quickly to flat iron, hot comb, wash, set, ponytail and pull back our naps. Learn how to wear our jeans the way that makes everybody comfortable except us. I know I did. I can't even remember why I was so quick to please everyone else. So quick to let go of my youth and be an adult because maybe then I could really make a change. So quick to let go of my past and make my own history. And yet so afraid to dream of my future. And as I grow I recognize that little girls who keep weak dreams will always be little girls and never become young women. So I've decided to commit to just this. In whatever future that decides to come I commit to believing in my own dreams. As cliché as that may sound or seem, I really do believe it's a first step. Dreams on paper or in poems are masks to the milky ways they represent. This summer I learned you can't keep them in notebooks and talk of them in circles. Dreams that wait in shoeboxes under bunk beds cry silently every night for the movement they could have become.

These dreams I spoke so often of and never acted on are green with envy as they learn about the Black Panther Party and Young Lords I tell myself I have to wait to become. What will I be at 21 that I am not now? I am 14 years old, which means I have 2 years to make a change before I can be put behind prison bars and that's not even guaranteed. Bobby Hutton was 18 when shot down for making his dreams happen, 16 when started seeing them come true. What am I waiting for, what are we waiting for? I am making my oath today to wear my naps free, and my jeans loose giving my womanhood some well-deserved space to breathe. I am committing to being comfortable in this skin, but even before comfortable, ready. Ready to let my dreams out from underneath my bed, out of my poems and notebooks, out of this room, and out of this brownstone, and most importantly out of this hood. I am committing to doing more than sitting at my windowsill and waiting for this to happen, I am committing to making it happen. Committing to apologizing through my actions to every single one of my ancestors who didn't sit around crying for what they lost, but stood up marching for what they could make happen. I've been blessed with the knowledge that women are not bitches; African Americans are not niggers, Latinos are not spics, and homosexuals are not faggots. So it is time for me to share that I am not a little girl, I do not have weak dreams. I am a young woman, my roots are dense and I recognize where they come from. My skin is smooth, and my thighs are thick and I recognize where that comes from. I have big dreams and even bigger plans. They say the youth shall set us free, and I commit to doing just that as soon as I free myself.

Performance Technique
Breathing, Movement, Exploration
Barbara Sellers-Young

Speak with Distinction: The Classic Skinner Method to Speech on the Stage
Edith Skinner

Performance Opportunities
Nuyorican Poets Café
This 30-year-old institution is one of the country's most highly respected arts venue for showcasing innovative poetry, music, hip hop, video, visual arts, comedy, and theatre.
Look for similar venues in your city.
www.nuyorican.org

Urban Word NYC™
A New York City organization helping youth discover their creative voice through written and spoken word, and by engaging them in important sociopolitical issues.
*Use this website to learn about **Teen Slam** contests taking place around the country.*
www.urbanwordnyc.org

Publishing Opportunities & Tools
Copyrighting
www.copyright.gov

Creative Kids Magazine
A national magazine featuring games, stories, and opinions by and for youth ages 8–14
www.prufrock.com/client/client_pages/
prufrock_jm_createkids.cfm

IndyKids
A "free paper for free kids" and a teaching tool on current events for grades 4–8
www.indykids.net

ISBN International Standard Book Number
The source for acquiring the 13-digit number that identifies published books internationally
www.isbn.org

Hip Hop Songwriting Contest
Take Back the Music, a campaign of *Essence* magazine, examines how Black women are depicted in popular music and seeks to promote balance in mainstream hip-hop's messages. In collaboration with the *Berklee College of Music,* the campaign hosts a contest to find the "next generation of hip-hop stars."
www.berklee.edu

Lulu Publishing
An online source for publishing and selling books, calendars, photography books, posters, and much more
www.lulu.com

Teen Ink
A national magazine, book series, and website for teen writing and art, distributed to English, creative writing, journalism, and art teachers around the country
www.teenink.com

Youth Communication
A publisher of "true stories by teens," Youth Communication helps young people develop their reading and writing skills toward making thoughtful life choices.
www.youthcomm.org

Epilogue
You Did Not Tell Me What to Say, You Inspired Me to Write

This unsolicited letter was written to Brotherhood/Sister Sol by an alumnus, and is offered as a closing illustration. Beyond giving Brotherhood/Sister Sol staff a "big up," the letter unintentionally, and eloquently, describes the approach and impact of our **Content, Perspective, Dialogue** Workshop Model.

Dear Brotherhood/Sister Sol,

I have been meaning to write this letter for quite sometime but have procrastinated not so much because I am lazy but because I fear my words can never do justice to what all of you have done for me.

I joined Bro/Sis about sophomore year of high school. I was a very confused youth. This was also about the time where I was acting out and rebelling against authority figures, especially in school. I felt that no adult outside of my mother cared about my future. School counselors did the minimum to make sure I graduated and went on to college and since I always did fairly well in school, no special attention was ever given to me. I hated school. At the time I did not know exactly why I could never bring myself to fully embrace Archbishop Stepinac High School. It wasn't until I started attending Lyrical Circle that I found out why. Lyrical Circle was the first place that I ever felt like people were paying attention to what I had to say because I was smart, talented, and had something relevant to say. I definitely was not using mainstream traditional mediums to address social, political, and personal issues, but that did not stop me and the fire I felt when I wrote.

At Bro/Sis I was introduced to my ancestors. I began to be immersed in a history I never knew existed. Jaques and Silvia would give us research assignments, and I was enthralled by the historical richness in each topic. For the first time in my life I was in a class where black was beautiful, smart, courageous, passionate, everything that I had been socialized to believe it wasn't. It is not so much that I faced overt racism in regular class (which at times I did) but omission and silence can sometimes have the same effect as blatant racism. Not having been sufficiently taught my people's history left me utterly confused and bitter. I was

123

angry; angry because I was not white I did not know where I belonged. Since I was born I was bombarded with images of whiteness, purity, and goodness. Everyone important was white: Jesus, George Washington, Abraham Lincoln, Rockefeller, Bill Gates, Superman, Batman, Spiderman, my doctors, dentists, and teachers. The message was clear. If I wanted to be successful and important I had to be white.

When I started LC I thought "finally, a place where I could be me and be important." I took what LC introduced me to and ran with it. I ran as fast and as hard as I could, only looking back to thank God I wasn't still back there. With my new insight on race and social differences I was able to understand why I hated school. Because I was one of the handful of Afro-Latinos in the school and no matter how much I tried I could never really fit in. I thank God every day that my eyes were opened, that I was welcomed and nurtured at Bro/Sis because the alternatives are horrifying. I either would have stripped myself of my ethnic identity or more likely dropped out and resented education for the rest of my life. Although I don't think dropping out of high school is necessarily a negative thing, but rejecting education is extremely detrimental to anyone's soul. Education systems can be racist but education itself isn't, and this is one of the most valuable lessons that I have attained through Bro/Sis. I love education; but I hate the paradigm that continues the Eurocentric model in schools, especially those full of black and Latino students.

So, what I want to say is thank you. Thank you for creating and helping maintain a space that saves people. It saved me and you might hear this often, maybe not often enough, but without this "thing" that you have birthed, I do not know where I would be. You did not give me an identity, you helped me search for it. You did not tell me what to say, you inspired me to write. And these are some of the greatest gifts anyone could ever receive. I shudder to think where I would be without each and every one of you. New staff, old staff, members, directors, people who I converse with, to people who smile and say hi, thank you all, I owe you one.

Your brother,
Enmanuel Candelario
Lyrical Circle, International Study Program (South Africa 2005), Writers' Collective Facilitator, Brotherhood Chapter Leader, B.A. Fordham University (2007)

• • • • •
ACKNOWLEDGMENTS

Why Did This Happen? is only made possible by the vibrant, intelligent, challenging, perceptive, and creative voices of the young sisters and brothers who trust my colleagues and I with their minds, bodies, and spirits. I know I speak for all Bro/Sis staff in offering them my gratitude, admiration, and respect.

This curriculum was nurtured by the experience and talents of extremely committed educators, mentors, big brothers and sisters, and collaborators. Thank you to all Bro/Sis staff, particularly those who have worked so closely with our teens: Cidra Sebastien, Wendy Arroyo, Silvia Canales, Nando Rodriguez, Orisanmi Burton, Valerie Caesar, DaMond Taylor, Enmanuel Candelario, Jacques Louis, and Evelín Aquino. Silvia and Valerie (*Art Herstory 101: The Power of the Personal Narrative*) and Orisanmi (*Identity, Power, Oppression*) provided great examples of Bro/Sis workshops. DaMond helped me describe how educators can turn the written word into performance art.

Akpé akakaka to the Co-Founders of The Brotherhood/Sister Sol and my partners for so many years, Khary Lazarre-White and Jason Warwin, for asking me to help develop an organization that is about more than education and enrichment, but is a way of thinking about and building more just communities—a way of life. I am a better educator, artist, sister, woman, leader for having accepted your offer.

Many thanks to Jane Lazarre for setting me off in the right direction, sharing insights from diverse writers, and careful editing. I am very grateful to Ruth Charney for helping me unpack The Brotherhood/Sister Sol model into a form that would be accessible to others. You also inspired me with your enthusiasm about our work.

I additionally extend my thanks to our Board of Directors, past and present, for their steady, dedicated support of The Brotherhood/Sister Sol.

Susan Wilcox
Harlem, NY
August 2008